128 Greatest
Stories
FROM THE

BIBLE

128 Greatest
Stories
FROM THE

BIBLE

Dan Harmon, Colleen L. Reece
& Julie Reece-DeMarco

BARBOUR
PUBLISHING

© 2005 by Barbour Publishing, Inc.

Print ISBN 978-1-61626-964-7

eBook Editions:
Adobe Digital Edition (.epub) 978-1-62029-460-4
Kindle and MobiPocket Edition (.prc) 978-1-62029-459-8

Published by Barbour Publishing, Inc., P.O. Box 719, Uhrichsville, Ohio 44683, www.barbourbooks.com

Our mission is to publish and distribute inspirational products offering exceptional value and biblical encouragement to the masses.

 Member of the
Evangelical Christian
Publishers Association

Printed in the United States of America.

For five special children
Alexa, Gabrielle, Sophia, Cade, and Ella
from Colleen and Julie

• • •

As author of the "guys" portion of this work
(one of the most wonderful, enlightening
and instructive research projects I've ever been given!),
I would like to dedicate my chapters to
all struggling Christians—men, women, and children.
Apart from Jesus, every man in the Bible was
a sinful, flawed individual,
but a creation of God with a purpose in God's plan.
So it is today with you and me!
Daniel

contents

Introduction. 11
Adam, the First Man. 13
Eve, Mother of All Humankind 13
Cain and Abel, Sibling Rivals 15
Noah, Spared from the Flood 16
Trying to Reach God with a Tower. 17
Abraham, Father of Israel 19
Lot, Neighbor of Wickedness. 20
Lot's Wife, Pillar of Salt 22
Sarai, Aged Mother. 24
Hagar and Ishmael, Abraham's Second Family. 26
Isaac Trusts His Father 28
Abimelech, God-Fearing King 30
Rebekah, Wife of Isaac 31
Jacob, Younger Brother 33
Esau, Cheated Brother 35
Rachel, Beautiful Sister. 36
Leah's Tender Eyes 38
Joseph, Son of Jacob 40
Reuben Saves His Brother 41
Potiphar's Wife, Temptress 43
Benjamin, Youngest Child. 45
Jochabed, Moses' Brave Mother 47
Miriam, Moses' Sister 49
Pharaoh's Daughter Adopts a Baby. 51
Moses, Leader of Israel 53
Aaron, Spokesman. 55
Zipporah, Shepherdess Wife. 56
A Multitude of Plagues. 58
Fleeing from Pharaoh 60
Walking through Parted Waters 62

The Coming of the Quails 64
Water in the Rock. 66
Moses and the Lord 67
A Golden Calf. 69
Moses Sends Out Spies. 71
Balaam and His Talking Donkey 73
Joshua, Moses' Successor. 75
Rahab, Harlot of Jericho 76
The Storming of Jericho 78
A Charge to the People. 80
Deborah, Wise Judge and Prophetess 82
Gideon's Small Army 83
Manoah's Wife, Mother of Samson 85
Samson, Foe of the Philistines 87
Delilah, Snare to Samson 89
Naomi, Mother-in-Law of Ruth. 91
Ruth, Moabite Girl 93
Boaz, Kinsman Redeemer. 95
Hannah Prays for a Child 97
Samuel, Promised to God 98
Saul, First King of Israel 100
Jonathan, Friend of David. 101
David and His Sheep 102
David, His Harp, and Jonathan 104
David Meets a Giant. 105
Michal, Daughter of Saul 107
Abigail, Wife of Nabal 109
Joab, Military Leader 111
Nathan, Bold Prophet. 112
Bathsheba, Mother of Solomon 114
Solomon's Solution 116
The Queen of Sheba Meets Solomon. 117
Jezebel, Idolatrous Queen 119
The Zerephath Widow and Elijah—
    Miraculous Meals. 121

Elisha Helps the Children 123
The Shunammite Woman Hosts Elisha 124
The Captive Maid 126
Hezekiah, Faithful King 128
Josiah, Boy King 129
Ezra and Nehemiah Rebuild Jerusalem 131
Hadassah, Queen of Persia 132
Job, Man with an Upright Heart 134
The Ideal Woman 135
Isaiah, Spokesman of God 137
Jeremiah, Youthful Prophet 138
Ezekiel's Visions 139
Daniel, Captive Prophet 140
Nebuchadnezzar, Babylonian King 142
Hosea, Cheated Husband 143
Joel and the Locusts 144
Amos, Farmer-Prophet 145
Jonah, Fleeing Prophet 146
Zechariah, Messianic Prophet 147
Matthew, Tax Collector Turned Apostle 148
Mary and Joseph, Family of Christ 149
Jesus Christ, Son of God 152
John the Baptist, Forerunner of Christ 153
John the Apostle 155
Peter, Fisher of Men 156
Jesus Heals Lepers 157
A Woman of Faith 159
Daughter of Jairus, Restored to Life 161
Philip Witnesses a Miracle 162
Judas Iscariot, Greedy Disciple 163
Thomas, Doubting Apostle 164
James, Brother of Jesus 165
Herod Antipas, Ruler of Galilee 166
Herodias, Wicked Wife of Herod 167
Salome Dances for Blood 169

The Canaanite Woman, Mother of Faith 171
The Ten Virgins and Their Lamps 173
The Most Terrible and Wonderful Days 175
Pontius Pilate, Coward 176
Pilate's Wife Has Troubled Dreams 178
Mary Magdalene Sees the Risen Christ 180
Barabbas, Prisoner Set Free. 182
Mark, Early Church Leader 183
Jesus and the Children 184
Jesus, the Rich Man, and Bartimaeus 186
Jesus Cleanses the Temple 188
The Poor Widow's Mites 190
Luke, Physician. 191
Elisabeth and Zacharias, Parents of
    John the Baptist 191
Anna and Simeon Meet Jesus. 193
Jesus Is Missing! 195
A Woman of the City. 197
Mary and Martha, Sisters of Different Priorities 198
Lazarus Lives Again 201
Zacchaeus, Man with a Changed Heart 203
The Woman at the Well 204
A Lad Shares His Lunch 206
The Woman Accused 207
Blind from Birth 209
Stephen, Christian Martyr 211
Paul, Missionary to the Roman Empire 212
Rhoda, Excited Servant Girl. 214
Lydia, Merchant of Purple 217
Timothy, Youthful Pastor 218

Fathers and mothers, husbands and wives, sons and daughters—the men and women of the Bible each have a story to tell. And between the covers of this book, you'll find the intriguing stories of more than one hundred individuals, in order of their appearance in the Bible. From Adam and Eve to Lydia, Mark, Peter, and Paul, these stories will inspire and encourage you as you live out your own story.

Adam was the first human, formed from dust and given God's own breath of life. He was placed in a beautiful garden God had planted in Eden. The Lord made Adam the caretaker of His garden and surrounded him with many wonderful plants for beauty and for food. God brought to Adam all the animals He had created, and Adam named them. Adam was free to enjoy this lovely garden. Only one restriction was placed on him: "Do not eat from the tree of the knowledge of good and evil," God warned. This tree was at the center of the garden.

God did not want Adam to live alone, so He put the man into a deep sleep, removed one of his ribs, and created a woman from the rib. He made the woman Adam's wife. Adam named her Eve.

Genesis 2:4–5:5

eve, mother of all humankind

Coolness patterned the garden into a mosaic of sunlight and shade. Soft footfalls announced the presence of One walking amidst trees and flowers. A voice, low but indescribably sweet, called, "Adam, where art thou?"

Trembling, the man and woman, formed and breathed into life by the Lord God Almighty, crept out of hiding. "Here, Lord," Adam whispered.

Eve shivered and clutched Adam's arm, seeking strength yet knowing he had none to give the helpmeet God had created from one of his ribs. The look on her husband's face when confronted by his Creator seared Eve's soul and burned like a hot coal that could not be extinguished. Fear. Shame. Regret. Brokenness. More than anything else, it showed her the magnitude of her folly. Why had she listened to the tempter? Worse, why had she caused her sinless husband to transgress God's law by encouraging him to do likewise?

If only they could go back just a few hours! The garden had been beautiful. God said they might eat fruit from all the trees in the garden, save one. If they ate from that tree, they would surely die. Neither Eve nor Adam questioned God.

Then the serpent appeared. "Ye shall not die. God knows that in the day ye eat your eyes shall be opened. Ye shall be as gods, knowing good and evil."

The tree before Eve glowed with beauty, offering food alluring above all others—and something more: wisdom, as the serpent promised. She reached out, took fruit, and ate. How wonderful! She plucked more and ran with it to her husband, who accepted it from her hands.

Innocence vanished. Aware of their nakedness for the first time, they hastily gathered fig leaves and formed aprons to cover themselves. When they heard God walking in the garden, they fled. What had seemed such a little thing at the time turned monstrous in their new knowledge of good and evil.

Eve shuddered, sickened by how easily she had turned away from right and chosen wrong. Half dazed, she heard Adam explaining to God that first Eve, then he, ate the forbidden fruit.

The Lord said to Eve, "What is this that thou hast done?"

Pierced to her innermost being by the sorrow in His voice, she said through dry lips, "The serpent beguiled me, and I did eat." Self-loathing filled her.

God cursed the serpent for what it had done. He condemned the tempter to crawl on its belly and said there would be enmity between him and womanhood forever. Then He turned back to Eve. "I will greatly multiply thy sorrow and thy conception; in sorrow thou shalt bring forth children; and thy desire shall be to thy husband, and he shall rule over thee."

Filled with misery and longing only to escape the presence of the One who had made her, Eve suffered even more when the Lord spoke to Adam. Because he had listened to his wife rather than keeping the commandment of God, he would toil all the days of his life. Thorns and thistles would hinder his work, and only by the sweat of his brow would he be able to bring forth food from the ground now cursed.

God made coats of skins and clothed Adam and Eve. He drove them from the garden of Eden, lest they eat of the tree of life and live forever. Eve sobbed uncontrollably, but cherubim and a turning, flaming sword made it impossible for Adam and her to ever again walk with God in the garden.

Time passed. God's promises remained sure. Adam worked hard, tilling the ground. Eve, the mother of all living, brought forth children in travail. Her heart tore with pain until she wondered if she would go mad when her eldest son, Cain, slew Abel, his younger brother, in a jealous rage.

With sorrow and joy, hard times and pleasant, the years rolled on. At times the lovely garden in which she and Adam once walked with God seemed remote, shrouded by the mist of many years. Yet as long as she lived, Eve never forgot her agony when she watched Adam face his Maker and recognized what havoc she had brought into the world by listening to the tempter rather than to God.

Genesis 2–4

cain and abel, sibling rivals

Cain was the oldest son of Adam and Eve. Abel was his brother. Cain farmed the soil; Abel was a shepherd. When they brought the Lord offerings of the fruit of their labors, God was not equally impressed. Cain's gift was a sampling of his crops—the Lord did not bless it. The blessing was reserved for the sacrifice of Abel—the choicest meat from his firstborn lamb.

This angered Cain, and the Lord chastised him for being angry and warned, "If you do well, you will be blessed. But if you do wrong, sin will overtake you." Ignoring the warning, Cain killed his brother in a rage.

Later God asked him, "Where is your brother?"

Cain retorted, "Am I my brother's keeper?"

The Lord already knew what had happened and condemned Cain to a life of endless wandering. Never again would the ground he farmed produce food.

"But I'll be homeless," Cain protested, "easy prey for anyone to kill."

So God placed a mark on Cain to warn people not to harm him. But for Cain, death would have been preferable to a roving existence in exile from the presence of God.

Genesis 4:1–16, 25

noah, spared from the flood

Judgment was at hand. Since the time of Adam and Eve, humans had multiplied, spread across the earth, and progressively turned away from God. "I am sorry I created them," God said of these violent and wicked people. "I will destroy every living creature on the face of the earth."

Only one man feared and obeyed God. His name was Noah. God told him of His plan to destroy both humans and animals with a great flood. But God gave Noah specific instructions for building an ark in which he, his family, and two each of every living creature would ride out the deluge.

The ark was like a huge barge, 150 yards long and three

stories high. Noah followed every detail of the Lord's commands, built the ark of strong wood, and sealed it carefully with pitch.

Finally the ark was finished. God gave Noah seven days to gather and board all of the animals. Then He made it rain for forty days and nights. The flood rose, covering the lowlands, then the hills, and finally even the highest mountains. The water was so deep that once the rain stopped, five months passed before the flood receded and the ark came to rest in the mountains of Ararat. It was many more months before the earth was dry again. Noah waited inside the ark until God told him to leave.

The first thing Noah did was make an offering of one of each of the sacrificial animals that had been in the ark. The Lord was pleased by this offering and promised Noah He never again would destroy every living creature. A rainbow appeared in the sky as a perpetual reminder of this covenant with Noah. God gave Noah dominion over all of the animals and plants. Everyone living on the earth today is descended from Noah and his sons Shem, Ham, and Japheth.

Genesis 5:28–10:32

trying to reach God with a tower

No one knew who first suggested it, although many laid claim to the bold idea. All who dwelled on the plain in the land of Shinar heard and understood, for the whole earth spoke one language.

"We must make bricks and burn them thoroughly so we will have stone," the leaders said. "We will use mud for mortar. Once our city and tower are completed, we will have a name and never be scattered all across the face of the earth."

If some felt it could never be done, they kept their doubts to themselves. Speaking out against the daring idea that had swept like a raging fire through the people was unwise. Especially when they were determined to build a city and a tower that would reach to heaven.

Preparations went forward, affecting old and young alike. One afternoon a small girl darted through the doorway of the simple home she and her family shared with their aged ancestor. "Grandfather, Grandfather!" Excitement flowed from her tunic-clad body. "Isn't it wonderful? A tower to heaven! Soon we will be able to see Jehovah Himself. What is He like, Grandfather?"

The old man sprang from the mat on which he had been reclining, his frail body strengthened by her words. "Do not speak of it, child!" he gruffly told her. "Never in the history of the world have men thought of doing such a thing. Say no more." He shook his head, drew his cloak about him, and sank back to the mat. "That I should live to see such a day! Child, I fear what the Lord God may do to those who think they can get to heaven by building a tower. The only way to reach Him is by obeying His laws."

The little girl stared at her grandfather and put one finger in her mouth. Her round eyes looked like two ripe olives in her warm, brown skin. "B–but everyone says—"

"Enough." Her grandfather shook his head and waved her away. "I will hear no more." He closed his eyes and turned on his side.

The child stared at him for a long time. Then she tiptoed outside and made her way to a big stone nearby. She sat down and drew circles in the dusty ground with one bare foot. The look on her grandfather's face troubled her. Never before had he spoken to her so fiercely. Was building the tower really displeasing to Jehovah, perhaps even making Him angry—as angry as Grandfather had been when she repeated what everyone at the common well was saying? If so, what was going to happen? Frightened at the idea, she jumped up from the rock and ran to find her mother and father.

Grandfather was right about Jehovah being displeased. One day when a great multitude was gathered together, something happened that changed life on earth forever.

"Why can't I understand what the people are saying?" the little girl cried, tugging at her mother's arm. All around them, people were speaking in different languages.

"I don't know," her mother said. Her father worriedly shook his head, looking as confused and afraid as the little girl felt. People immediately began gathering their children and fleeing from friends and neighbors who had instantly become strangers, speaking words she couldn't understand.

"There will be no city and no tower," Grandfather said. "Come, we must go."

The child trudged after him, still clinging to her mother's arm. At least she could still understand her parents and Grandfather. Even if she couldn't talk with anyone else, she knew they would take care of her.

"Therefore is the name of it [the city] called Babel. . . ."

Genesis 11

abraham, father of israel

Generally regarded as the "father of the Jewish nation," Abraham is a wondrous example of how God works His will in impossible situations.

The life story of this grand Old Testament patriarch would pale the most intricate plots of Hollywood screenwriters—and it all really happened! God told Abraham to break away from his father's family and go to a new land. God promised to make a great nation of Abraham's descendants and bless them. "I will bless those who bless you, and curse those who harm you," the Lord told him. So began the formation and trials of God's chosen people.

There was an unhappy chasm between Abraham and his

nephew Lot. But when Lot and his household were captured by a warring kingdom, Abraham and a military force of three hundred soldiers rescued them. God made a covenant with Abraham and promised that his descendants would be as numerous as the stars in the sky—even though Abraham's wife, Sarah, was too old to bear children. In fulfillment of this promise, God gave them a son in their old age. They named him Isaac.

Nowhere was Abraham's obedience so severely tested as in the mountains of Moriah where the Lord commanded him to sacrifice Isaac. Abraham prepared the altar, gathered the wood, lit the fire, bound the unsuspecting youth, and placed him on the altar. Abraham drew a knife and was actually poised to kill his son—so committed was he to God—when an angel of the Lord stayed his hand at the last instant.

Abraham had proven he would keep nothing from the Almighty, not even his cherished son. In return, God reiterated His pledge to make Abraham's descendants as numerous as the stars in the sky and as the grains of sand along the ocean shore.

Sarah lived to be 127, Abraham, 175, and they were buried in a cave in the field of Ephron in Canaan.

Genesis 11:27–25:10

lot, neighbor of wickedness

When God sent Abraham and his wife, Sarah, into the land of Canaan, they were accompanied by Abraham's nephew Lot. In time, Abraham and Lot prospered in the new land. As their flocks grew larger, however, their shepherds quarreled over pastureland. To make peace, Abraham gave Lot his choice of land to settle on, so Lot moved east to the fertile Jordan River valley. There he pitched his tents near Sodom, a city of evil people. Meanwhile, Abraham settled in Canaan.

Tribal warfare soon visited the Jordan Valley, and Lot and his household were taken captive by a conquering army. When Abraham got word of this, he took several hundred men and pursued the marauders. In the aftermath of a brilliant surprise attack, Abraham's men scattered the enemy and rescued Lot and the other captives.

Fifteen years later, Lot found himself in even greater trouble. The cities of Sodom and Gomorrah had become so evil that God planned to destroy them. Lot was sitting near the city gate of Sodom when two men (who were actually angels) approached. Lot insisted that they stay with him and share a meal. After supper they were roused to find that Lot's house was surrounded by all the men of the city. The evil men called for Lot to send the two men outside. The mob had wicked intentions. Lot was afraid for the strangers, and to pacify the mob, he offered to send his two virgin daughters out to them. "Do not harm my guests," he pleaded. Lot's refusal to release the strangers to them angered the would-be molesters. They rushed the door of the house, but the two angels struck them blind!

The angels instructed Lot to take his family and leave immediately because the Lord's destruction of Sodom was imminent. Naturally, Lot's family resisted. The angels had to take Lot, his wife, and his two daughters by the hand and lead them out of the city. As they fled in the predawn hour, God rained fiery sulfur down on the cities of Sodom and Gomorrah, which were consumed together with all their inhabitants. Lot and his family were saved. All except for Lot's wife. She could not resist turning to look back at the destruction of her home. At that very spot she was turned into a pillar of salt.

This sordid story does not end here. After their escape from Sodom, Lot and his two daughters lived in a cave. The daughters worried that they would never be married and have children. So they made their father drunk and slept with him. The two children who came forth from these incestuous unions were ancestors of the nations of Moab and Ammon, future enemies of Israel.

Genesis 11:31; 12:4; 13:1–14:16; 19:1–38; Luke 17:28–30

Lot, nephew of Abraham, hastened home at eventide and called to his wife, "Make haste! Prepare unleavened bread."

The mistress of the household looked up, startled by his excitement. She caught sight of two strangers entering the house behind him. "Who—?"

Lot lowered his voice. "As I sat at the gate of the city, two angels came to me. I bowed and prayed that they might tarry all night in this, their servant's house. At first they said nay, they would abide in the street, but when I pressed upon them greatly, they agreed."

Angels! The woman's mouth fell open, but she hurried to do her husband's bidding, pressing her daughters into service, as well.

Before the household lay down for the night, the men of Sodom encircled the dwelling place, demanding the strangers be brought to them.

Lot stepped outside and closed the door. He entreated them not to do wickedly. He said, "Behold, I have two daughters which have not known man; let me, I pray you, bring them out unto you, and do ye to them as is good in your eyes: Only unto these men do nothing; for therefore came they under the shadow of my roof."

Anger raged inside his listening wife. Was he mad, to sacrifice his own daughters for the sake of the two sheltered under his roof? If they were indeed angels, could they not protect themselves from the rabble outside the door?

Lot's pleas proved useless. The crowd pushed toward Lot and intended to break the door. Before they could do so, the strangers pulled Lot inside, shut the door, and smote the mob with such blindness they could not find the door.

Weak with relief, Lot's wife sank back to her pallet and

clutched a shawl around her. She heard the visitors say, "Hast thou here any besides? Son-in-law, and thy sons, and thy daughters, and whatsoever thou hast in the city, bring them out of this place; for we will destroy this place, because the cry of them is grown great before the face of the Lord; and the Lord hath sent us to destroy it."

Destroy the city? The listening woman plucked at her shawl with nervous fingers. Lot went out and told his sons-in-law they must get up and leave at once. They laughed and mocked him, refusing to believe the Lord would destroy the city.

In the morning the angels hastened Lot. "Arise, take thy wife and thy two daughters which are here, lest they be consumed in the iniquity of the city." While Lot lingered, the angels laid hold upon his hand, and his wife and daughters' hands, and led them forth, the Lord being merciful. One angel warned, "Escape for thy life; look not behind thee, neither stay thou in all the plain; escape to the mountain, lest thou be consumed."

Lot pleaded that they might instead flee to a little city and that it would not be overthrown. The angel agreed and again urged them to make haste.

The sun had risen by the time Lot and his wife entered Zoar. Terrible sounds came from Sodom and Gomorrah, even from the plain and all that grew on the ground. Lot's wife could not stand it. From her position behind her husband, she wailed with grief. Only two of her daughters had been saved. The others had remained in Sodom with their husbands. In her despair, she turned her face toward the way they had come, either ignoring or forgetting the commandment the angel had given not to look back. Fire and brimstone fell from heaven, devouring everything and everyone in its path.

When Lot and his daughters sought the wife and mother who had accompanied them, nothing remained but a pillar of salt.

Genesis 19

Hunched and intense, Sarai listened to the remarkable tale her husband, Abram, related. "The Lord came to me in a vision. He told me He was my shield and my exceeding great reward. I cried to him, 'Lord, God, what will Thou give me, seeing I go childless? Thou hast given me no seed, and lo, one born in my house is mine heir.'"

" 'This shall not be thine heir,' the Lord said. 'Look now toward heaven, and tell the stars, if thou be able to number them. So shall thy seed be.'"

"You believe this to be true?" Sarai tried to keep her words calm, although her heart pounded with doubt.

"Yea, for He showed me many other things."

A ripple of scornful laughter escaped Sarai's lips. "I am an old woman, Abram," she proclaimed. "My childbearing days—if I ever had such—are long past." Bitterness crept into her voice.

"I only know what the Lord has said." Abram rose and departed.

They spoke no more of the matter, but it lay between them, a living thing that permitted Sarai no rest. Why God had restrained her from bearing a child, she did not know. Why, then, had Jehovah given her husband the vision? Perhaps it was no vision but the product of Abram's longing for a son.

When Sarai could no longer bear the weight pressing on her, she went to her husband. "Behold now, go in unto my maid; it may be that I may obtain children by her."

Abram hearkened to Sarai's voice. He took the Egyptian maid Hagar to be his wife, and she conceived. At once, Hagar began to despise her mistress.

Sarai saw it. Fury raged within her. Had she not given Hagar to her own husband that God's promise might be fulfilled? Now the younger woman dared set herself up against her mistress. It was unbearable.

"My wrong be upon thee," Sarai upbraided Abram. "I have given my maid into thy bosom, and when she saw she had conceived, I was despised in her eyes: The Lord judge between me and thee." She held her breath, waiting his judgment.

"Behold, thy maid is in thy hand; do to her as it pleaseth thee."

Sarai dealt harshly with Hagar, who fled from her wrath for a time.

When Abram was ninety-nine years old, the Lord appeared and gave him a new name: Abraham. He established an everlasting covenant to be a God unto Abraham and his seed. He also gave Sarai a new name. Henceforth, she would be no longer Sarai, but Sarah. She would have a son, who would be called Isaac, and become a mother of nations. Abraham fell upon his face and laughed in his heart. A man have a son at one hundred, with a wife of ninety long years? Never in the history of the world had such a thing happened.

Sarah could not and would not believe she would bear a son in her old age, but she denied laughing, for she was afraid. When she conceived and began to be great with child, Sarah pondered how such a thing could be. After long, empty years, God had granted her the desire of her heart.

Abraham was a hundred years old when Sarah delivered Isaac, whose name means "laughter." And she said, "God hath made me to laugh, so that all that hear will laugh with me. Who would have said unto Abraham that Sarah should have given children nourishment? For I have born him a son in his old age."

The child grew, and on the day Isaac was weaned, Abraham made a great feast. Sarah had not conquered her hatred of Hagar. She demanded that Hagar and her son Ishmael be cast out. Sarah rejoiced when the bondwoman and young Ishmael went away into the wilderness, not realizing God would one day make the young man ruler of a nation.

Sarah lived to be 127 years old. She never stopped marveling that God had sent a son into her barren life long after hope of such a thing had unfolded its wings and flown away.

Genesis 12, 15–18, 20–21, 23

I hate being a handmaid, the Egyptian girl, Hagar, thought. _Especially for one like Sarai. She is old and ugly. I am young and alive. Why must I serve and obey her?_ She pressed her lips together, and her resentful thoughts rushed on. Nothing she did ever proved good enough for her faultfinding mistress. The plight of one who served had never weighed down on her so heavily as right now. Sarai became more demanding with each passing day.

Hagar smothered mirth, fearful of being discovered at the secret listening post where she learned much more than her mistress knew. Abram had just finished relating some impossible dream he called a vision from God.

Sarai's derisive laughter echoed in Hagar's heart. The idea! What kind of God thought a man of Abram's age could father a child? Pah! Her contempt grew. Even if he were able, why would Sarai conceive now when she hadn't in all these years? Hagar shook with silent laughter, but in the following days, she caught a brooding look in her mistress's eyes. She learned Sarai planned to give her handmaid to Abram.

At first the idea repelled Hagar; then cunning rose. A wife, even a second wife, held a more important place than a servant. Even though she never conceived, anything was better than her present position. She shrugged. Her wishes in the matter meant nothing. A handmaid did her mistress's bidding.

When Hagar knew she had conceived, triumph flooded through her. She made no attempt to hide her disdain of Sarai,

26

childless and barren. As carrier of Abram's son and heir, she felt she would also have his protection. She did not. He gave Sarai permission to deal with her as she would. Many a bitter tear Hagar wept before fleeing into the wilderness on the way to Shur. Not until she reached a fountain of water did she stop and wonder what would become of her and her unborn child. There an angel of the Lord found her.

"Whence camest thou? Wither wilt thou go?" he asked.

Rubbing her eyes to make sure she was not dreaming, Hagar replied, "I flee from the face of my mistress, Sarai."

The angel told her she must return and submit herself to Sarai. He promised to multiply Hagar's seed exceedingly. He also told her she was with child and would bear a son. "The Lord has heard thy affliction," he said. "Name the child Ishmael"—which means "whom God hears"—"because the Lord hath heard thy affliction. And he will be a wild man; his hand against every man, and every man's hand against him."

Hagar returned to Sarai. Ishmael was born when Abram was eighty-six years old. His delight in his son made up for some of what Hagar suffered from Sarai, who daily grew more resentful of her handmaid and the boy. Things worsened when Ishmael was fourteen and Sarai, now Sarah, delivered Isaac. What would become of Hagar and Ishmael?

They soon found out. The next morning, Abraham, as he was called, rose early, put bread and a bottle of water on Hagar's shoulder, and sent her away with Ishmael to wander in the wilderness of Beersheba.

When the water was spent, she cast her son under one of the shrubs and went a far distance off. "Let me not see the death of the child." She lifted up her voice and wept.

The angel of God called to Hagar out of heaven. "What aileth thee, Hagar? Fear not; for God hath heard the voice of the lad. Arise, lift up the lad, and hold him in thy hand; for I will make him a great nation." God opened Hagar's eyes, and she saw a well of water. She filled the bottle and let the lad drink, holding the promises of the angel of God deep in her heart.

As Ishmael grew, God was with him. The boy dwelled in the wilderness and became an archer. Hagar took him a wife out of the land of Egypt, and great was her joy. Outcasts from the tents of Abraham they might be, yet God had protected her and the child of her body. Twice an angel had promised Ishmael would be a great nation. One day it would come to pass. Blessed be Jehovah!

Genesis 16, 21

isaac trusts his father

Several years after Ishmael was born, God changed Abram's name to Abraham and Sarai's name to Sarah. He told them they would have many children. Abraham laughed. He was one hundred years old. Sarah was ninety. How could they have children?

One day as he sat in the tent door on the plains of Mamre during the heat of the day, three men appeared. Abraham offered them food and water. One of the strangers told Abraham that he and Sarah would have a son.

Sarah, who was inside the tent, laughed at the idea. She, have a son at her age? Impossible!

With God, nothing is impossible. Isaac was born, just as God had told Abraham and Sarah. He grew into a fine young lad.

Early one morning, Father saddled his donkey. "Come," he told his son Isaac and two servants. "God has called me to the mountain. We must take wood and fire for the burnt offering at the place God has told me."

A trip with Father? How exciting! Isaac's heart pounded, and he flew to get ready. Yet all through their journey, he wondered why Father looked so sad. He longed to ask, but something in his father's face kept him silent.

Three days after leaving their home, Abraham said to the servants, "Stay here with the donkey. My son and I will go worship and then come back here."

Isaac trotted up the trail, his shorter legs trying to keep up with his father's long steps. Father carried the fire and a knife. Isaac felt proud that his father let him carry the wood.

"Father," Isaac said.

"Here am I, my son."

Isaac felt puzzled. "Behold the fire and the wood, but where is the lamb for the burnt offering?" he asked.

"My son, God will provide a lamb for a burnt offering," Father Abraham told him, and they both went on together.

When they reached the mountaintop to which God had directed them, Abraham built an altar where they could worship God, as was their custom. He laid the wood on it. Then he tied Isaac up and put him on top of the wood.

"What is happening?" Isaac cried. He looked all around, but there was no lamb in sight. He looked back at his father, trying to understand. Where was the lamb God was supposed to provide for the burnt offering? Why had Father tied him and placed him on the altar?

Abraham picked up the knife. For a moment, Isaac felt afraid. Then he remembered how much his father loved him. Even though everything was strange, Isaac trusted his father. His heart told him that his father would never harm him.

Suddenly an angel called from heaven. A ram was caught in the bushes by his horns. Abraham untied his son, caught the ram, and offered him as a burnt offering.

"We shall call this place Jehovahjireh, which means 'in the mount of the Lord it shall be seen,' " Abraham told Isaac.

The angel of the Lord called out of heaven a second time. He said because Abraham trusted his Father in heaven so much, God would bless him with so many children and grandchildren that they would be like stars in the sky! All the nations of the earth would be blessed because Abraham had obeyed God.

Abraham and Isaac went back to the servants and the donkey. It was time to go home.

Genesis 22

The Hebrew woman Sarah was very beautiful, and Abimelech, king of Gerar, took notice. She had been living in Abimelech's country with Abraham for some time. Abimelech thought they were brother and sister and so brought Sarah into his household to be one of his wives, as was the accepted custom of the time. But Abimelech was a God-fearing man. He was devastated when the Lord came to him in a dream and revealed that Sarah was in fact Abraham's wife!

"But I did not know I was doing wrong!" Abimelech protested. "They both told me they were brother and sister."

Happily, the Lord had not allowed Abimelech to touch Sarah after she had entered his house. "Return Abraham's wife to him," the Lord said. "He is a prophet, and he will pray for you. But if you do not return her, you and everyone in your household will die."

Early the next day, Abimelech told his servants what had happened. He summoned Abraham and demanded to know why the couple had deceived him. Abraham explained: When he and Sarah entered Gerar, he was not sure it was a land of God-fearing people. He was afraid some man enticed by Sarah's beauty would kill him in order to obtain her as a wife. So Abraham persuaded Sarah to pose as his sister. She was, after all, his half sister because they had the same father.

Rather than venting his fury against Abraham, Abimelech gave him an offering of livestock, slaves, and money. He gave him the best land in Gerar on which to live. Of course he returned Sarah to him unharmed. Abimelech wanted everyone to know he had not come near Sarah. During the time Sarah was in Abimelech's household, the Lord had made the king impotent. But after Abraham prayed for him, God restored Abimelech to full health.

Abimelech is a notable example of a God-fearing man who, when confronted with his mistake, went out of his way to seek reconciliation with the people he had harmed and, most important, reconciliation with the Lord.

Genesis 20

---

rebekah, wife of isaac

The eldest servant of the house of Abraham knelt by a well of water near the city of Nahor in Mesopotamia. Ten laden camels waited nearby. "Oh Lord God of my master, Abraham, I pray Thee, send me good speed this day, and show kindness unto my master." He paused. Could he fulfill the oath he had made to his master? Abraham had told him an angel would go before and lead the trusted servant to a kinswoman willing to accompany him to the tents of Abraham and become wife to Abraham's son Isaac. How would a humble servant know her?

He continued, "Behold, I stand here by the well. The daughters of the men of the city come out to draw water. Let it come to pass that the damsel to whom I shall say, 'Let down thy pitcher, that I may drink'; and she shall say, 'Drink, and I will give thy camels drink also': Let the same be she that Thou hast appointed for Thy servant Isaac."

Before he had finished speaking, Rebekah, a fair young virgin, went down to the well and filled her pitcher. She curiously eyed the stranger and his well-laden camels. He asked for water and she gladly gave him her brimming pitcher. "I will also draw water for the camels," she told the stranger. Pitcher after pitcher she drew and poured into the trough so the camels could quench their thirst.

When they finished, the servant gave Rebekah a golden earring of half a shekel weight, two bracelets, and ten shekels' weight of gold. He asked her father's name and if lodging could be had in his house.

"I am daughter of Bethuel, the son of Milcah, whom she bore unto Nahor," she proudly announced. "We have both straw and provender enough, and room to lodge in."

Nahor, brother of Abraham! The servant bowed his head and worshipped the Lord, praising Him for His leading.

Rebekah ran and told those of her household concerning the strange encounter. Her brother Laban immediately went for the stranger and welcomed him. While they sat and ate, the servant told everything that had transpired. He told how rich Abraham was in flocks and herds, in servants, silver, gold, and beasts. He related how a son had been born to Sarah in her old age and how Abraham had sent his eldest servant to find a kinswoman to become Isaac's wife.

Rebekah's heart leaped within her, especially when the man confessed he had prayed for God to lead the right woman to the well and was even given the words she should say! Humility at having been selected by God as Isaac's wife filled her, and she breathlessly waited for her family to speak.

"Wilt thou go with this man?" Laban and Bethuel asked Rebekah.

"I will." They blessed her and sent her on her journey.

Rebekah whiled away the weary traveling hours wondering what her husband-to-be would be like. When she first saw Isaac, she found him pleasant to look upon. His eyes held love, and she became his wife.

Twenty barren years later, when Isaac was sixty, the Lord blessed Rebekah with twins: Esau, hairy and red, then Jacob. Esau turned to hunting and the field; and Jacob, whom Rebekah loved more, dwelled in the tents. She secretly rejoiced when Esau sold his birthright to his younger brother for bread and a pottage of lentils. Had not Jacob been born with one hand on Esau's heel, symbolizing that he, not his elder brother, should rule?

Isaac grew old. Rebekah's ambitions for Jacob soared. She commanded him to disguise himself as Esau, take the savory meat Isaac loved, and receive the blessing that belonged to the older son. Fear soon replaced her joy. The cheated Esau threatened to kill Jacob, and Rebekah sent her favorite son away, weeping bitterly. What had she done? What good was her life if Jacob chose the wrong woman for his wife? She took comfort when Isaac charged Jacob to pass by the daughters of Canaan and go to Rebekah's father and take a wife from among the daughters of Laban, her brother. Yet again and again she remembered the bitter enmity she had sown between her sons because of her terrible desire for Jacob to rule.

Genesis 24, 27

jacob, younger brother

Jacob came into the world clutching his twin brother's heel. This was symbolic of struggles to come. Jacob contended with his older brother, Esau, over the birthright and the blessing of their father, Isaac. Jacob won, but only through deception. The story of the enmity and eventual reconciliation of these patriarchs is told later in this book in the account of Esau.

After stealing the blessing from Esau, Jacob fled to northern Syria to live with his uncle Laban. During the journey he stopped one night to sleep and used a rock for a pillow. There Jacob had a dream of a ladder that reached from earth to heaven. Angels were climbing up and down on this ladder. In the dream the Lord promised Jacob that his descendants would cover the earth and that He would be with Jacob in his travels.

When Jacob awoke, he was frightened and said, "This is the house of God and the gate of heaven!" He named the place Bethel and promised that if God would take care of him, he would always worship God and return to the Lord a tenth of everything he ever received.

Welcomed into his uncle Laban's household, Jacob fell in love with Laban's daughter Rachel. He told Laban he would work for him seven years if Laban would give him Rachel's hand in marriage. Laban agreed.

The seven years flew by, or so it seemed to Jacob. He was head over heels in love with Rachel. When Laban arranged the wedding, he gave his older daughter, Leah, to be Jacob's wife instead of Rachel. Jacob furiously protested. Laban explained the custom—the oldest daughter married first. He promised to let Jacob marry Rachel, too, but only if Jacob would work another seven years! Jacob agreed and eventually had both daughters as wives. But he always preferred Rachel.

God saw that Leah was unloved and allowed her to have children, while Rachel was unable to conceive. Jacob had six sons by Leah, two other sons by Leah's maid, and two sons by Rachel's maid. Finally God remembered Rachel and let her have a son of her own; his name was Joseph. Later Rachel died giving birth to her second son—Jacob's twelfth—who was called Benjamin.

In time, relations between Jacob and Laban became very strained. Laban was not happy that Jacob's livestock multiplied and grew healthier than the other herds. Jacob yearned to return with his household to his homeland, but Laban realized that the Lord's blessings on Jacob over the years had had a positive effect on his own fortunes. Ultimately Jacob and his family fled in secret. Laban and his men chased and caught them, but conflict was averted and Jacob and Laban made a pact and parted peacefully.

During the journey back to his homeland, Jacob wrestled with God, who appeared in the form of a man. All night they wrestled, and Jacob's hip was thrown out of joint in the struggle, but he was not defeated. As daylight approached and the man began to leave, Jacob refused to let Him go until he received a blessing from the divine opponent.

"From now on," the man said, "your name will be Israel, because you have wrestled with God and with men and have won."

Genesis 25:19–32:32

Esau and Jacob were twin brothers, sons of Isaac and Rebekah. Their relationship was not a peaceful one. Even inside their mother's womb they clashed. "Two nations are inside your womb," God explained to Rebekah. "One will be stronger, and the oldest will serve the youngest." Esau was delivered first, with Jacob following behind, clutching his brother's heel. And as God had said, Esau was left out of the Hebrew lineage despite his birthright as the firstborn son.

It happened this way: Isaac came to favor Esau as the boy grew because Esau was an excellent hunter and brought his father wild game to eat. Jacob, more inclined toward domestic life, became Rebekah's favorite. One day Esau came home from the wilds extremely hungry and asked for some of the stew Jacob was cooking. "Trade me your birthright for it," Jacob said. Famished, Esau unthinkingly swore to give Jacob his birthright.

Some time later this verbal theft of Esau's birthright came into effect when Rebekah and Jacob tricked Isaac, who was old and blind, into granting his blessing to Jacob. Isaac had sent Esau into the wild to kill an animal and prepare the meat in Isaac's favorite way. Isaac promised that after he ate the wild game, he would bless Esau. Rebekah overheard Isaac's words and told Jacob to kill some goats nearby. She used them to prepare the special meal and sent Jacob into Isaac's tent dressed in Esau's clothes so he would smell and feel like Esau. Isaac would never know the difference. Jacob served his father the meal and received the blessing of the firstborn son in place of Esau.

The ruse worked. Jacob received the blessing that by right should have been given to Esau, the true firstborn. Part of the blessing was the headship of the family. "May all who curse you be cursed, and all who bless you be blessed," Isaac said.

Shortly afterward Esau returned with the game, prepared it

the way his father liked, and took it to Isaac hoping to receive his blessing. But Isaac could not revoke the blessing he had already given Jacob, even though he had made a mistake. So Esau was designated to serve his younger brother just as God had foretold. Esau was furious and vowed to kill Jacob as soon as their father died. So Jacob fled to Haran to live with their uncle Laban.

Many years later, Jacob sought to reconcile with Esau. Imagine Jacob's fear when Esau came to meet him with an army of several hundred men! Jacob sent a generous offering of livestock to Esau. As they approached each other, Jacob bowed low seven times to pay homage to his brother. Esau forgot his wrath and tearfully ran to embrace and forgive Jacob for his deception.

Pardon can rarely be as moving as when Esau reconciled with the brother who had stolen his birthright.

Genesis 25:21–34; 26:34–35; 27:1–28:9; 32:3–21; 33:1–16; 36:1–19

rachel, beautiful sister

Of the many tasks necessary to keep her father's household and holdings running smoothly, Laban's younger daughter, Rachel, best liked caring for the sheep. Sometimes her older sister, Leah, chided her about it. "Why can't you be like other women, instead of always wanting to be off with a smelly bunch of animals?" She pulled a long face. "You won't see me chasing after unruly lambs or rams and ewes that have to be pulled from thickets." Leah delicately pinched her nostrils with a thumb and forefinger. "No man will seek your hand when you smell like dirty, wet wool."

Rachel only laughed. What did she care? Still young in years, she had plenty of time to find a husband. She refrained from saying so. For some reason, Leah had waited year after year for love to seek her out but remained unbetrothed. Rachel loved her sister and could not understand why men passed Leah by.

Perhaps if she hadn't been so busy tending sheep, Rachel would have spent more time peering into a pool of water, noticing the reflection of a beautiful, well-favored young woman—whose charms made Leah's tender eyes pale into insignificance by comparison.

One day Rachel and her flocks came to a well in the field, as was her custom. A great stone lay rolled over the well's mouth. When all the flocks of sheep were gathered, the stone was rolled away and the shepherds watered the sheep. This day a strange young man stood nearby. Rachel hesitated, feeling hot color steal into her smooth cheeks and not knowing why.

To her surprise, he came straight to her. "You are the daughter of Laban, son of Nahor?"

"Why, yes. I am Rachel." Her heart pounded.

"I have traveled far. I am your kinsman Jacob, son of Isaac who married Rebekah, sister of Laban." He kissed Rachel, lifted up his voice, and wept.

Rachel broke free, stared, then ran to tell her father. More than the exertion of running made her heart beat more wildly than ever. That unruly member continued to leap in the most unmaidenly way all through the month Jacob abode with Laban and his family. Rachel hid it as best she could and refused to even discuss Jacob with Leah.

At the end of the month, Jacob struck a bargain with Laban. "Rachel has found favor in my sight. I will serve thee seven years for her hand."

Laban saw the chance to gain an expert workman. "It is better that I give her to thee than to another man: Abide with me."

For seven years, Jacob served Laban, never suspecting the scheme in the other's cunning mind. When the marriage feast finally came, Laban exchanged Leah for Rachel! The next day, Jacob bitterly accused him of treachery. Laban replied that in their country the firstborn must wed before the younger. "You shall also have Rachel if you vow to serve seven more years," he promised.

Rachel, who had been distraught at her sister's marriage to

Jacob, felt hope stir in her heart. Yet it seemed too much to ask. Fourteen years for the love of a maiden? Such a thing had never before been done in her country.

"I will serve," Jacob huskily told Laban, his gaze steady on Rachel. Nothing could have shown Rachel better how much she was loved—far more than her sister Leah ever could be. It sustained her through the years when Leah bore strong sons and a daughter, but Rachel remained barren.

But God had not forgotten Rachel. Finally she conceived and bore a son. She praised the Lord, crying, "God hath taken away my reproach." She called her son Joseph, meaning "He shall add." She also said, "The Lord shall add to me another son," and kept the foreknowledge close in her heart.

Rachel died birthing Benjamin, her second son, and was buried on the way to Bethlehem. Her name lives on as a mother in Israel who loved her husband, her children, and her God.

Genesis 29–31, 35

leah's tender eyes

Leah, daughter of Laban, hated the elder-sister role life had forced her to play. Why must a woman with a loving heart be condemned to idleness simply because no man had yet spoken for her? Must she forever be compared with another, always unfavorably?

Leah loved Rachel. Sometimes she exulted in the girl's young beauty. More often she despaired. In her deepest soul-searching, she honestly admitted it was unreasonable to believe anyone would pass fair Rachel by in favor of her elder sister. Her lip curled. The few who had, did so with an eye to Laban's holdings, not for love of his daughter. She would have none of them.

The day their kinsman Jacob came, Leah felt a stirring

deep inside. Here was a man who more than fulfilled her secret dreams. Strong, gentle, his very presence made Leah's heart throb with longing, then grow numb at the look in his eyes. There was no room in his heart for anyone but Rachel.

In spite of the knowledge, Leah refused to accept defeat. Had she not seven years to show herself as worthy as Rachel, if not as beautiful? Even when months fled into years and the marriage feast day drew near, a slim hope remained. Would Laban, powerful as he was, break tradition and allow his younger daughter to wed first?

In a twinkling, everything changed. Leah could scarcely grasp the rapid change in her life. She, not Rachel, became Jacob's wife. Triumph blotted out all else—until the next morning. Hope of his loving her vanished when Jacob discovered Laban's deceit. Leah wondered if she would ever forget the sight of his face when he beheld her, not Rachel, for whom he had toiled so long. Like a slim, keen blade, it plunged into her heart, twisting and turning when her father extracted Jacob's vow to serve another seven years in exchange for Rachel. Now she lay sleepless, passionately wishing her husband lay by her side and not her sister's. She could imagine them whispering, perhaps blaming her as well as Laban. At times she writhed, wishing she had never seen the man who had become her husband, then passionately clutching at the shreds of his love with both hands in an attempt to convince herself one day he would care.

When the Lord saw Leah was not loved, He blessed her with children. With each, she felt Jacob must surely learn to love her, especially when her sister remained barren. Instead, Jacob's heart lingered with Rachel, his first and only real love. Six strong sons and one beautiful daughter Leah gave her husband, rejoicing in each, clinging to the fading vision of one day possessing Jacob's heart.

After the birth of Dinah, God hearkened unto Rachel and she conceived. Jacob's countenance wore joy far beyond any he had ever shown over the arrival of a child by Leah. Again hurt flayed his first wife.

Leah faced greater conflict once Rachel delivered her son Benjamin. Jacob, now called Israel, could not hide the fact he cared far more for Joseph and Benjamin, Rachel's sons, than his other sons and daughter.

Though she desperately tried, Leah never recaptured the brief triumph she had known on her marriage day. As in girlhood, her fair young sister's shadow lay over Leah all the days of her life.

Genesis 29–31

joseph, son of jacob

Was he arrogant or just sincerely proud? Whichever, Joseph grated on the nerves of his ten older brothers. He clearly was their father's favorite. Jacob had even given him a special gift of a lavishly colored coat.

Not only so, Joseph had the audacity to tell his brothers about his dreams—stories of symbolic bundles of wheat and celestial bodies which implied that the brothers would someday pay Joseph homage.

One day as Joseph's brothers tended sheep, they saw the boy coming across the field. "Here comes that dreamer," they scoffed and conspired to put an end to Joseph's insolence. They would have killed him but for the mercy of Reuben, their oldest sibling. He proposed they throw Joseph into a dry well. This they did. But when a caravan of Ishmaelites en route to Egypt happened by, the brothers sold Joseph to them as a slave. Thus the lineage of Abraham was diverted to this foreign land.

Although only a slave, Joseph prospered in Egypt. His master, Potiphar, the commander of Pharaoh's palace guard, placed Joseph in charge of his entire household. But this favored position was not to last. Potiphar's wife, impressed by the handsome young man, tried to seduce Joseph. When he refused, she connived to have him jailed.

But still the Lord brought Joseph back to prominence, this time through his timely interpretation of Pharaoh's troubling dreams. Joseph told Pharaoh that his dreams indicated there would soon be seven years of abundant crops in Egypt followed by seven years of famine. Pharaoh heeded this warning and stored up reserves of grain for the coming hard times and made Joseph the governor of the whole country—even though he was still a slave!

A dramatic family reunion came when, during the famine, Joseph's brothers journeyed to Egypt to buy food. Of course, they did not recognize Joseph, and he played a hard game with them. The youngest brother, Benjamin, who was Jacob's favorite, was set up as a thief. This warranted severe punishment in Egypt. But Judah, one of the older brothers, assumed the blame for Benjamin. Joseph was so moved by this that he revealed his identity and tearfully welcomed them. And the brothers paid him homage just as the dreams had said. Jacob's entire household relocated to Egypt during this difficult time, and Joseph took care of them.

In time, however, the descendants of Jacob would become slaves of the Egyptians, because no one like Joseph remained in power to look after their interests. This set the stage for the dramatic exodus of the children of Israel and their odyssey to the Promised Land.

Genesis 37, 39–50

reuben saves his brother

The suggestion to kill Joseph, put him in a pit, and say that an evil beast had eaten him found favor among most of the brothers. "Here comes the dreamer," they said to each other when they spotted Joseph's colorful coat a long distance away. "We shall see what becomes of our younger brother's dreams that we will become his servants. That young boy will not rule over *us*."

Joseph's brother Reuben refused to kill Joseph. "Shed no blood," he told the others. "Just leave him in the pit." He didn't tell them that he meant to sneak back, free Joseph, and return him to their father.

Joseph had no idea how much his brothers hated him or what they meant to do. He was just there to find out if they were well so he could go home and report to his father.

"What are you doing?" he cried when they seized him and tore his coat of many colors from his body. "Why are you treating me so?"

His protests didn't stop them. They threw him into a pit that held no water and left him there. All Joseph's cries for help did no good. Soon, only the dry, hot land heard his frantic pleas to be released.

Joseph's brothers sat down some distance away to eat bread, well pleased with having rid themselves of the boy who said they must bow down to him. Before long, a company of Ishmaelite travelers came by, bound for Egypt. Their camels were loaded with spices, balm, and myrrh.

Judah, one of the brothers, had a bright idea. "Joseph is our brother," he said. "What good is it to kill him and have to hide what we have done? Let's sell him to this caravan. That way we won't have his blood on our hands. Besides, we'll make some money." The others—except Reuben, who had gone back to deliver Joseph from the pit—thought it was a fine idea.

Before Reuben could return alone to the pit where Joseph lay, some Midianite merchantmen passed the brothers. They lifted Joseph from the pit and sold him to the Ishmaelites.

When Reuben got to the pit, he softly called his brother's name. "Joseph?"

His only answer was silence, deep and frightening.

"Joseph?" Reuben called again, looking into the pit. It was

empty! His brother was gone. Reuben tore his clothes and went back to his brothers. What could they tell Father Jacob?

The brothers decided they must cover up what they had done. They killed a goat and put some of its blood on Joseph's beautiful coat of many colors. The brothers traveled the long miles back to their home and their father, who waited for a son who would not come. When they reached Jacob, they told him, "We found this. Tell us, please, is it the coat you made for Joseph?"

Jacob took the stained coat from them. He said, "It is my son's. A wild animal surely has torn Joseph to pieces." He wept bitterly for the son he thought was dead.

Joseph was not dead. God had helped Reuben stand up to his brothers and save Joseph's life. While Jacob mourned his lost son, Joseph had been sold to Potiphar, the captain of the guard for the Egyptian pharaoh.

Genesis 37

potiphar's wife, temptress

Potiphar's wife eyed the well-favored young slave her Egyptian husband had acquired some time before. A slow smile crept over her painted lips. What an open-faced youngster this Joseph was! Her sluggish blood, jaded by many conquests, stirred. Young men always attracted her. She licked her lips like a giant cat savoring its prey long before securing it.

"Where did you find him?" she asked.

Potiphar, captain of the guard and highly respected, smiled at her. No one dared inform him of his wife's indiscretions. To do so meant risking terrible punishment. Even if one spoke, Potiphar would not believe. His fierce, possessive love blinded him to the wickedness thinly veiled to all but him.

"An interesting story." He glanced at Joseph and paused. The woman reclining on a couch saw a flicker of pain in the young slave's face. "You may go," Potiphar told Joseph, who gracefully walked away. Watching Joseph brought another gleam to the wife's eyes.

"He seems—healthy."

"He's far more than that. He has served so well I have put him in charge of all my affairs. Never have I had such an overseer." A strange look crossed Potiphar's face. "Since he took charge, my holdings have increased." He laughed. "Joseph says his God has blessed this house and my fields."

"His god!" A quick swing of her feet brought the woman to a sitting position. "Which one? Osiris, god of the underworld?"

Potiphar shook his head. "No. Joseph worships one he calls Jehovah. He says there are no other gods. Anyway, the boy was born to his father's favorite wife in later years. The old man loved Joseph more than his half brothers and made him a coat of many colors. It made the others hate him. Things worsened when Joseph told of a dream that when interpreted meant he would rule over his family and they would one day bow down to him."

"I should think they would!" Interest whetted, Potiphar's wife disdainfully flicked a hand. If she chose to pursue her interest in the young man, he needn't think she would bow to him—or any other.

"Most of the brothers wanted to kill him, but Reuben, the eldest, intervened. He convinced them to shed no blood but to cast the boy into a pit. Later they sold him to a band of Ishmaelites who brought him to Egypt. A good day for us," he added.

"A good day," she agreed, fingers stroking her silken draperies.

Potiphar's wife bided her time, taking care to act circumspectly in front of her husband but casting meaningful glances toward Joseph on every possible occasion. He seemed not to notice them. It baffled her. Was he so innocent he could not see her invitation? Or so clever he chose to ignore it? The thought sent scarlet flags to her cheeks.

One day when Potiphar was not home, his wife summoned Joseph and sent away her maids. Her heart raced with excitement. "Come." She gestured to the couch where she lay.

Joseph refused, saying he could sin against neither his master nor his God.

Potiphar's wife hid her rage and shrugged. He would lay aside his scruples soon enough. Yet time after time, Joseph continued to refuse her advances. His reluctance goaded her on until she determined to break his will.

One afternoon when no other men were in the house, Joseph once more turned down her invitation. She snatched his garment. He fled, leaving it in her hand. Enraged at being rejected, she cried in a loud voice, "See? The Hebrew came in to mock me. When I cried out, he fled, leaving his garment." She told the same tale to her husband when he came home. None of the household dared deny her lies.

Potiphar's wrath kindled against the young man he had trusted with all he possessed. He comforted his sobbing wife and had Joseph thrown into prison. He never knew his wife rejoiced, then decked herself out for her next conquest.

Genesis 39

benjamin, youngest child

Benjamin watched his brothers ready themselves for the long journey that lay ahead of them. After seven years of bountiful harvests, trouble had spread over every country like a smothering woolen blanket. The food supply was already low, and who knew how many failed crops lay ahead? Something had to be done.

In the midst of their worry, good news came. It ran throughout the land of Canaan like a river in flood. "There is corn in Egypt. People from every country are hastening there to buy."

Jacob called his sons together. "Why do you stand there looking at each other? There is corn in Egypt! Hurry down there and buy for us, so we may live."

Benjamin's heart pounded with excitement. Egypt—the mysterious country about which he had heard so much. He could hardly wait to see it.

"Benjamin, you will remain here with me," Jacob said.

Questioning Jacob's decision was not permitted, but the boy's desire to see Egypt was so great that he could not control himself. "I must go with my brothers, Father!" he burst out.

A lightning flash of anger came into Jacob's face. "Hold your tongue! I have said you shall stay."

"Yes, Father." Benjamin dug his toes in the dusty ground. It was hard being the youngest son. It seemed his father never let him do any of the things his brothers did. "Just because a wild beast killed Joseph doesn't mean I'm going to get hurt," he said, too low to be heard. "That was a long time ago. Besides, what could happen with ten strong brothers to take care of me?"

For one wild moment, Benjamin considered sneaking away to follow his brothers. He could stay just far enough behind so as not to be discovered until they were too far away to turn back. The corners of his mouth turned down. No. He wouldn't. He had already angered his father today by questioning his wishes. Instead, he asked, "Why does Egypt have food when we don't?"

Some of Jacob's anger died. "I do not know, my son."

What Jacob didn't know was that God had spoken to Joseph, now second in command over all of Egypt. Seven years earlier, the pharaoh had dreamed about cattle and corn, and no one could tell him what his dream meant. God told Joseph that it meant there would be seven years of plenty followed by seven years of famine. When Joseph shared this information with Pharaoh, he listened to Joseph and stored food during the good harvests.

Only nine of Benjamin's brothers came back with food. Simeon had been arrested. Joseph—whom none of his brothers recognized—sent word that Benjamin must come to Egypt to prove that the brothers were not spies!

Jacob refused to consent until the food was almost gone. He wept when he said good-bye to his excited son. When Benjamin got food in Egypt, Joseph had his men hide his silver cup in the sack. It was part of Joseph's plan to make it look as if Benjamin had stolen the cup. When Benjamin and his brothers started on the journey home, Joseph's men caught up with them, searched Benjamin's sack of grain, and found the cup. Then they told the brothers that because Benjamin had stolen the cup, he must return to Egypt and be Joseph's slave!

"Father Jacob will die if Benjamin does not come home," his brothers protested.

Joseph was very glad to hear that his father was alive, and he told his brothers who he really was. "I have forgiven you," he said. "I believe God allowed me to be sold so that all these years later, the family wouldn't starve. Here are fine clothes for you." He turned to Benjamin, who stood staring. "Here are three hundred pieces of silver for you."

Benjamin was speechless. His eyes shone as brightly as the coins! And when Jacob and his family moved to Egypt, Benjamin rode on top of a wagon and was the happiest of all!

Genesis 42–44

jochabed, moses' brave mother

Strange thoughts troubled the king of Egypt. He was new to the throne, and his perplexities rose daily. Some he could shunt off to his advisors, but not the ever-growing problem he encountered each time he gazed on his subjects. The children of Israel who dwelled in the land were fruitful. They increased abundantly. They multiplied until the land was filled with them. He abominated them all and, worse, feared what they might become and do.

The king said to his people, "Behold, the people of the children of Israel are more and mightier than we. We must deal wisely with them. If war should come, they would join our enemies and fight against us, so get them up out of the land." The corners of his mouth drew down, and he swished his royal robes.

At the king's orders, taskmasters were appointed to afflict the children of Israel with their burdens. They were held in bitter bondage and forced to build for Pharaoh treasure cities, Pithom and Raamses. In mortar and brick and all manner of service of the fields they were made to serve, to endure the hardship or drop and be beaten. Death offered the only freedom. For four hundred years, they were enslaved. Yet the more the Egyptians afflicted them, the more the Israelites multiplied and grew.

Could nothing stop them? The king ordered the Hebrew midwives to perform a terrible task. At the time of delivery, daughters might live; every son must be killed. The midwives feared God. They saved the male children, in spite of their orders to the contrary.

The king called for them and demanded, "Why have you done this thing?"

The midwives said to Pharaoh, "The Hebrew women are lively, not like the Egyptian women. They deliver before we arrive." God dealt well with the midwives and the people continued to multiply and grow mighty.

Determined not to be outwitted, Pharaoh charged all his people, saying, "Every son that is born you shall cast into the river, and every daughter you shall save alive." A wailing in Egypt rose that assaulted the ears of its inhabitants as the dark river waters swallowed up countless innocent male children.

About this time, a daughter of the house of Levi, married to Amram, also of the house of Levi, conceived. Jochebed bore a son. She refused to comply with the king's edict, believing somehow the child must be saved. For three terrifying months she concealed her child, but the time came when she could no longer keep him without discovery.

"I cannot let my baby be destroyed," she whispered into the shawl that held him. A plan born of desperation formed. She made an ark of bulrushes, a floating basket daubed with slime and pitch to keep the water out. Jochebed carefully tucked the child in its depths, covered him, and eased it into the flags by the brink of the river that had claimed the lives of so many other babies.

Why must such things be? her aching heart silently cried. *Lord God of Israel, protect my little son.*

"Stay hidden by the river," Jochebed commanded her daughter, Miriam. "Watch the ark carefully. We must know what happens to your brother." She stumbled away, knowing she had done all she could to save her child but wondering how she could stand the pain.

Some time later, her daughter, Miriam, rushed home. "Mother, mother!" Her childish, treble voice rose to a high, excited pitch. "Pharaoh's daughter found the ark." She stopped for breath. "You are to nurse the baby—for wages!"

Never in her wildest dreams had Jochebed envisioned such an outcome. The best she had hoped was for a kindly soul to rescue the child and conceal him as she could no longer do. Jochebed fell to her knees. "Blessed be the Lord God of Israel," she cried. "Jehovah has heard my prayer and this day delivered my son by His mighty hand." A little later, she settled down, nursing the son doomed to die by Pharaoh's decree but spared by God for a mighty, world-changing role.

Exodus 1–2

---

miriam, moses' sister

Small Miriam carefully held the tiny bundle her mother had placed in her eager arms. Eyes round, she touched the miniature fingers and gently stroked the baby's soft cheek. "Mother, he is so beautiful. Surely God will not allow him to die." She hopefully looked up at Jochebed, busy with bulrushes, slime, and pitch.

Her mother sighed. "I hope not, child. Yet other beautiful children have died by order of the wicked pharaoh. If only we could leave this land of bondage! How long, oh Lord, how long?"

The familiar cry for freedom, kept low to keep from disturbing the sleeping baby, rang loud in Miriam's ears. Child that she was, yet she recognized the longing. It echoed in her heart. "If we are Jehovah's chosen people, why does He allow us to be oppressed?" she fiercely demanded.

"Hush, Miriam. It is not for us to question the ways of Jehovah. Besides—" Jochebed's nimble fingers stilled, and a faraway look came to her eyes. She lowered her voice to a whisper, and her daughter leaned closer. Even walls had ears these days. No one knew how idle words crept into the wind, but speaking of certain subjects meant harsh punishments, even death.

"My child, one day a deliverer will be sent, one to lead God's people out of this land and into a place of freedom."

A deliverer. In a passion she could not describe, Miriam fiercely whispered, "When will the deliverer come?" Her gaze dropped to the little brother she loved with all the feelings of her young heart. "Mother, why does Jehovah not send the deliverer now, when we need him so badly?"

"We cannot know the ways of the Lord," Jochebed sadly told her. She continued smearing the ark with slime and pitch. "There, it is finished. When it dries, it will be the finest small boat anyone could ask for. We shall pray for it to safely carry your brother to someone who will care for him."

A little later, Miriam watched her mother place the baby in his new floating cradle. Awake now, he made no cry. Jochebed laid the ark on the water, admonished her daughter to keep watch, and trudged away.

For a time nothing happened. Then a rustle warned Miriam someone approached. She made herself small in her hiding place.

"Why, what is that?" someone said.

Miriam gasped and peeked from shelter. The pharaoh's daughter stood a short distance away. Her maid drew the basket with the baby from the water. The compassion in the look Pharaoh's daughter bestowed on the crying baby gave Miriam courage to spring forth and ask if she should bring a Hebrew nurse for the child. On winged bare feet, she sped to her mother with the gladsome news.

Miriam became a fine woman, respected by her people. She served as a prophetess, skilled with the timbrel and dancing, singing praises to the Lord and rejoicing over the goodness of God. Yet in spite of her calling, she at one time allowed jealousy to influence her and spoke against Moses for marrying an Ethiopian woman. "Has the Lord spoken only by Moses?" she and Aaron demanded. "Has He not also spoken by us?"

A strangled cry arose from Moses and Aaron.

They speechlessly pointed.

Miriam looked down at her hands and tottered. Her skin had turned white as snow from leprosy. "Oh God, what have I done?" she wailed.

Moses cried to the Lord on her behalf, imploring Him to remove the curse. The Lord in His goodness hearkened unto Moses' pleadings, but for seven long days Miriam was shut out of the camp for her rebelliousness. After she rejoined the others, she again became respected and never tired of telling how Jehovah saved Moses, the deliverer who freed the Israelite people from Pharaoh's cruel hand and led them to the Promised Land.

Exodus 2, 15; Numbers 12

pharaoh's daughter adopts a baby

In the eyes of those who dwelt in Egypt, Pharaoh's daughter had everything a girl or woman could desire. The finest silks and cloth of gold clothed her. Jewels lay unworn in costly caskets, simply because of their number. The very stars in the heavens could not outshine Pharaoh's daughter when her maidens decked her out.

Only one thing she did not have: peace of mind. Naturally compassionate and kindhearted, she raged when her father the king ordered the Hebrew midwives Shiphrah and Puah to kill all sons of the Hebrew children when they were called to serve in their office. She secretly rejoiced when the midwives did not obey the commandment. How clever of them to say the Hebrew women were more lively than those of Egypt and had already delivered the children by the time the midwives came!

One day the daughter of Pharaoh went to the special place in the river where she washed herself. She walked along the river's side, anticipating the clean, fresh coolness awaiting in the secluded spot she had made her own. Yet today a foreign presence had entered her domain. Something rocked among the flags.

"Bring it to me that I might behold it," Pharaoh's daughter ordered her maid. The servant obeyed. Pharaoh's daughter bent low over the retrieved object. "Why, it's an ark, fashioned of bulrushes, daubed with slime and pitch! How came such a thing to my bathing place?"

Nimble fingers opened the ark. Pharaoh's daughter's eyes grew wide at the sight of the contents. A tiny wail issued from the basket. Fear clutched the girl's heart. She sent a hasty glance back toward her maidens. "Be gone! I will remain here for a time."

Giggling and fluttering, they hastened to obey. When only her maid remained, Pharaoh's daughter drew forth the babe. Compassion filled her soul. "This is one of the Hebrews' children." Color fled from her face. "What shall we do? If father knows the small one lives, he will order the babe thrown into the river, as so many before him. His life will be snuffed out like a candle in the wind." She held the tiny boy close to her beating heart, and he nestled against her. "It shall not be! He is mine."

A small voice beside her whispered, "Shall I go and call a nurse of the Hebrew women, that she may nurse the child for you?"

Pharaoh's daughter whirled, the babe still clutched close to her bosom. Liquid brown eyes stared out of a smooth face. Something in their depths silently assured Pharaoh's daughter she had nothing to fear from the Hebrew girl before her. "Go," she commanded.

With a fast-beating heart, she waited the short time that felt like hours. The Hebrew child returned, holding an older woman by the hand. The suffering of the Israelite people shone in the woman's eyes, but her gaze met that of Pharaoh's daughter honestly. Again came a feeling of trust. "Take this child away and nurse it for me, and I will give you wages," Pharaoh's daughter ordered. She noted the way the woman's gentle hands accepted the wrapped babe, the instinctive cuddling that came only from a woman who possessed great love for all children.

"His name is Moses," Pharaoh's daughter said. "For I drew him from the water. He shall be my son."

Level gaze met level gaze. The woman smiled and bowed. A strange, mystical expression crept into her eyes. "It is well." She bowed again and walked away with her charge.

Pharaoh's daughter stared after her, wondering. The Hebrew nurse's face had filled with such radiance that in spite of her rude clothing, she appeared lovelier by far than the pharaoh's daughter in all her glory.

Exodus 2

moses, leader of israel

He was born in the worst of times. Not only were his people, the Hebrews, slaves in Egypt; the pharaoh had decreed that because the slaves were multiplying so fast, every newborn Hebrew boy must be drowned in the Nile. Therefore, Moses' mother kept him hidden for the first three months of his life. When she could keep him no longer, she set him adrift in a reed basket along the edge of the Nile River. The basket was discovered by Pharaoh's daughter. After Moses' own mother raised him, he was adopted into the royal family.

One day, young Moses saw an Egyptian beating a Hebrew slave. Moses rushed to his kinsman's defense and killed the Egyptian. Fearing he would be reported and executed, Moses buried the Egyptian in the sand and fled to the land of Midian. There he married and settled down to work as a shepherd. But God had a very important task in mind for Moses. God's people, the Hebrews, were slaves in Egypt and desperately needed a leader to confront Pharaoh and demand their release.

Moses was quietly tending his father-in-law's livestock on Mount Sinai one day when God appeared to him in a burning bush. God commanded the exile to return to Egypt and lead the Hebrews to freedom.

Moses protested, "Who am I to do this?"

"I will be with you," the Lord replied and commissioned Moses to go in the name of the great "I Am." Then Moses complained that he was not a good orator. So God agreed to let Aaron, Moses' older brother, be his spokesman. God spoke to Moses, and Moses relayed God's messages through Aaron.

Moses and Aaron appeared boldly before Pharaoh. The Lord punished Pharaoh's stubbornness by singular means, and the Hebrews ultimately escaped under the leadership of Moses. The Red Sea waters opened, and the people were free. This story is an unparalleled epic. Of equal impact is its sequel: The freed masses were mutinous and contentious. Even Moses' own brother, Aaron, and his sister, Miriam, joined in their antics. As this horde wandered toward the Promised Land, God, through Moses, gave them the Ten Commandments and other laws.

Moses was faithful to the Lord. But there was an occasion in the Zin Desert when Moses disobeyed the Lord. This failure bred disrespect for God among the people, so God did not allow Moses to enter Canaan, the land he had promised to Israel. Before Moses died, however, God let him glimpse the land from the top of Mount Nebo across the Jordan River from Canaan. So Moses died in Moab, and his successor, Joshua, led the Hebrews into Canaan.

Exodus; Leviticus; Numbers; Deuteronomy

aaron, spokesman

When God commanded Moses to lead the Hebrews out of Egypt, Moses begged to be excused. "I am not an eloquent speaker," he complained. So God allowed Moses to engage his older brother, Aaron, to be his spokesman. Aaron transmitted to the people God's words to Moses.

Moses and Aaron's encounters with Pharoah in which God demanded, "Let My people go," are among the most dramatic portions of scripture. They provide riveting lessons in divine patience and punishment. God performed astonishing miracles through Moses and Aaron—such as turning a stick into a snake and changing the Nile River into blood. God sent a string of catastrophes upon the Egyptians, which culminated in the historic night when death visited the firstborn son of every Egyptian household. Still Pharoah refused to release Israel or respect their God. Aaron is not always mentioned in the narrative of the Bible, but he was always at Moses' side.

The exodus of Israel climaxed with their passage through the Red Sea and God's annihilation of the Egyptian army that had stubbornly followed them. Then years passed when Israel wandered in the wilderness and sorely tried the patience of Moses and Aaron. As leaders, they did as the Lord commanded, but the people repeatedly lost faith. When thirsty or hungry or facing a hostile army, the Hebrews complained bitterly. Yet God met their needs in miraculous ways. One would think the wandering Hebrews, more than any other people in history, would have believed, because they repeatedly saw God's power and faithfulness—yet they doubted and rebelled against their leaders.

Aaron was also given a task beyond that of spokesman. God made him the high priest and instructed that he be lavishly and meticulously attired for this position. Only Aaron and his descendants were authorized to offer sacrifices for the Israelites. Yet even Aaron lost faith. On one occasion, when Moses was alone on Mount Sinai for an extended period with the Lord, the people became restless and persuaded Aaron to make for them the image of a god. So Aaron melted gold into a calf-shaped idol for the people to worship. They believed it was the god that had brought them out of Egypt!

This misplaced allegiance and loss of control led to bloodshed, and Moses had to intercede before the Lord on behalf of the people. In response, God forgave them and promised to remain with Israel. But because of Aaron's flawed leadership and the people's diminished respect for God as a result, God did not allow Aaron to enter the Promised Land.

When the time came for Aaron to die, the Lord instructed Moses to go with his brother to the top of Mount Hor. There Moses removed Aaron's beautiful robe and placed it on Aaron's son, Eleazar, thus designating him as the next high priest. Aaron died, and the Israelites spent thirty days in mourning for their leader and high priest.

Exodus; Leviticus; Numbers; Deuteronomy

zipporah, shepherdess wife

Reuel, the priest of Midian (also called Jethro) had seven daughters. Zipporah, "the bird," was one of them. A maiden's life in the land of Midian was not easy. Time after time when the girls came to the well to draw water, fill the troughs, and water their father's flocks, unfriendly shepherds drove them away, mocking, laughing, and calling out crude jests. Even Zipporah, strong and unafraid, could not stand against them. They were forced to wait a long time before watering the sheep.

One day Reuel's daughters came home to their father, driving their flocks and arriving far earlier than was their custom.

"How is it that you are home so soon today?" he inquired.

A babble of voices arose, excited and incoherent.

"Silence!" their father commanded. "Speak one at a time so a man can comprehend what it is you wish to convey."

His daughters obeyed, but their eyes and faces shone with the startling occurrence that had taken place earlier in the day.

"We took the flock to the well for water," one began.

"The shepherds came as usual to drive us away," another said.

"Suddenly an Egyptian came; we know not from whence." The story grew even more amazing. "He dealt harshly with the shepherds and delivered us out of their hands."

"That isn't all," several chorused. One added, "The stranger also drew water enough for us and watered the flock that we might not have to do it."

Reuel marveled and said unto his daughters, "Where is he? Why is it that you have left the man? Call him that he may eat something."

Weary from his long journey, sick at heart over having slain an Egyptian he found smiting his Israelite brethren, Moses gladly accepted the kindly priest's offer of shelter and sustenance. He had left Egypt after a Hebrew who was fighting with another asked, "Who made you judge over us? Do you intend to kill me as you killed the Egyptian?" At that moment, Moses realized his deed was known and he was in great danger from Pharaoh. Here in Midian he could abide in content.

Zipporah looked on Moses with favor. Unlike the men of her own country, his deep gaze sent warmth to her skin and longing to her heart. The day her father gave her to be Moses' wife brought joy beyond belief. So did the birth of their son.

Moses insisted the child be called Gershom and said, "I have been a stranger in a strange land."

Zipporah tried hard to understand the things her husband told her. Still she wondered. What manner of man saw burning bushes that were not consumed? Or talked with Jehovah, as a man to a friend?

Greater questions were yet to come, then a long separation. After traveling with her husband to Egypt, where his brethren were enslaved, Zipporah's heart ached when Moses sent her back to her father in Midian to wait there with their sons, Gershom and Eliezer. Tales came to them of the many plagues visited on the Egyptians because of the hardness of Pharaoh's heart and the release of the Israelites after the death of the Egyptians' firstborn. More stories rode the wind: the parting of a sea to provide dry land on which Moses and his followers trod; the rush of water once they were safe that drowned the attacking Egyptian army; the children of Israel fed manna in the wilderness.

At times Zipporah wondered if she would ever again cast her gaze on the man who had captured her love but held true to a higher calling. At last, great happiness came. Jethro heard of what God had done for Moses. He took Zipporah, Gershom, and Eliezer to the tents of Moses in the wilderness. Jethro rejoiced for the goodness the Lord had done and said, "Now I know the Lord is greater than all gods; for in the thing wherein they dealt proudly, he was above them." Zipporah's joy knew no bounds, and she marveled at what a mighty leader her husband, Moses, had become.

Exodus 2, 18

a multitude of plagues

"Look at Moses," a sturdy Hebrew boy said to his companions. "See how strong he is? My father says Jehovah has chosen

Moses to lead us out of this cursed land. We will be delivered."

"Our people have been talking about being delivered since before we were born," his friend scoffed.

"Watch your tongues!" a third boy warned. He looked around to make sure no one was near enough to overhear their conversation. He had no desire to feel the sting of the whip—or worse—that was dealt out to those who dared criticize Pharaoh.

He lowered his voice to a whisper. "We will be delivered. The Lord God promised."

"I will believe it when we shake the dust of Egypt off our feet forever," the second boy declared. "I am sick of slaving for the Egyptians. If Moses is so great, why doesn't he call down curses from heaven on those who oppress us and grind us into the dust?"

The boy's question hung in the minds of many. Every day conditions worsened. First they had been forced to make bricks, and then to gather straw for the bricks and still make as many bricks as before. Pharaoh's men missed no opportunity to beat those who could not keep up, even those who were old and sick. Fierce hatred filled the hearts of the Hebrews who suffered such treatment, especially the young.

"How long, oh Lord?" was the cry of every heart. "How long before we are delivered?"

The three boys were forced to work so hard that they had little time or desire to talk. Just when they didn't think they would ever be delivered, a multitude of plagues came to the land. Moses pleaded with Pharaoh to let the children of Israel go, but he would not. Not when for seven seemingly endless days, the rivers, streams, and ponds flowed with blood instead of water, and the stench of dying fish filled the air. Not when the frogs came. Hundreds of frogs. Millions of frogs. They got into houses, beds, and ovens. Not with the lice or flies. Not even with the death of all Egyptian cattle, although not one of the Israelites' cattle perished!

"Surely Pharaoh will let us go!" one of the three friends told the others at the end of another wearisome day.

"He promises to free us, but when the plagues end, he refuses," another said. "I wonder what Jehovah will do next?"

So did the Egyptians. Both people and beasts were stricken with terrible boils. Thunder and hail came such as had never before been seen. It broke every tree of the field, except in the land of Goshen, where the children of Israel dwelled. Again Pharaoh promised to free them but broke his vows again and again, through plagues of locusts and darkness so thick that even a candle would not stay lighted.

It wasn't until after a night that the three boys and no one in Egypt would ever forget that Pharaoh finally let the people go. But what a terrible cost! Safe within homes marked with the blood of a lamb so the angel of death might pass over them, the Hebrews heard the wailing of those whose firstborn children died because of the hardness of Pharaoh's heart. He even lost his own son. The next morning, Pharaoh told Moses and Aaron to take the people and their flocks and herds and go serve the Lord.

Soon the great exodus began. No one was happier than the three friends.

Exodus 7–12

fleeing from pharaoh

"Make haste, children, lest we be left behind," the Hebrew parents urged.

"Pharaoh has changed his mind many times. If we do not hurry and go, he may do so again."

It was all the prodding needed to encourage even the smallest children to do all they could to help get ready for the departure of the children of Israel to a land God had long promised they would occupy.

"What if the wicked pharaoh comes after us?" a small girl

fearfully asked her big brother. "What will we do?"

He put his arm around her. "Don't you worry, little sister. Jehovah will not allow Pharaoh to harm us. Didn't He send plagues so we could be free? And give us Moses and Aaron to lead us through the wilderness?"

"Will they protect us?" she wanted to know.

"Yes. Now run and help Mother finish preparing for our journey."

The little girl scampered away, leaving the boy to wonder whether he really believed the words he had said to comfort his sister. Should Pharaoh decide to send soldiers after the travelers, would Moses and Aaron be able to protect the Hebrews from the long and cruel reach of the king?

The boy glanced down at his hands and flexed his scarred fingers. He turned them palm side up and looked at the thick calluses that marred them. When he was first pressed into the service of Pharaoh and sent to work among those making bricks, his hands had been free from the ugly marks of unwilling service. He winced, remembering how his hands had blistered and bled from the torturous work. Even applying the oil of olives had not healed the pain that continued until at last the blisters turned to calluses.

Anger flared within him. "No matter what happens, we will be better off than we are now," he said, still staring at his mutilated hands. "I would rather die trying to be free than to live another day in slavery!"

A call from his father interrupted his bitter thoughts.

"Come, my son, you are needed."

Once again the boy marveled at the change that had come over his white-haired father. Ever since Moses announced that his people were free, the old man's face had appeared years younger. Eyes dulled by years of oppression shone as bright as the stones tumbled and tossed by the river and left gleaming on its banks. Shoulders bent from the weight of countless bricks were proudly squared.

A prayer of thankfulness filled the boy's heart and replaced some of the anger he felt because of the past. It was the dawn of a new morning. He must not allow concern over what lay ahead to dim the anticipation of a new life. Something his father had taught him and his sister long ago crept into his mind. *"Never forget. Jehovah is more powerful than all the armies and all the kings who sit on thrones."*

His sister had asked the question that had been burning on his lips but held back because he knew it would grieve his father: "Then why doesn't He make Pharaoh let us go?"

Their father had replied, "I do not know Jehovah's will or plan any more than I know how He hung the moon and stars in the night sky or causes the sun to shine. I only know that His promises are sure. Someday we will be free."

Now the long-awaited "someday" had come. The boy shook off his troubled thoughts and hurried to help his father get ready.

Exodus 13

walking through parted waters

"Why is Moses taking us into the wilderness by the Red Sea?" a boy asked his friends as they trudged along beside heavily laden camels and donkeys. "It is far shorter to go through the land of the Philistines."

"Moses says God told him that if our people see the war in the land of the Philistines, they might be tempted to go back to Egypt." A second boy picked up a stone and fired it away from the slowly moving caravan snaking its way to the Promised Land.

"*I'm* not going back!" a third announced, dark eyes flashing. "I've felt the Egyptian lash on my back for the last time."

A murmur of agreement swept through the group. Young as they were, not one had escaped cruel treatment by their Egyptian masters.

"God is leading us," the oldest of the little band reminded.

Excitement brightened his dust-streaked face. "Every day He goes before us in a pillar of cloud, and every night in a pillar of fire. We need not fear."

Yet even as he spoke, the pharaoh and his servants were plotting against the children of Israel. "Why did we let them go?" they raged.

"Make ready my chariot," Pharaoh ordered. "Gather all the chariots of Egypt, with captains over each one, all the armies, and all the horses. We shall overtake the Israelites and bring them back to serve us again."

The pursuers found the children of Israel camped by the Red Sea.

"The enemy is upon us!" the people screamed. "Moses, why did you lead us here to die? Better for us to serve the Egyptians than to perish in the wilderness." Even the boys who had vowed never to return into bondage shivered and watched wide-eyed as Pharaoh's forces came closer and closer.

"Fear not," Moses told the people. "Stand still and see the salvation of the Lord. Never again shall you see the Egyptians you have seen today. The Lord shall fight for you, and you shall hold your peace."

"Look! The pillar of cloud has gone behind us and brought darkness between us and our enemies," a boy cried. "They cannot see us."

Moses lifted his rod and stretched his hand out over the sea. All that night the Lord caused the sea to go back by a strong east wind. The waters divided, leaving a path of dry land in between!

"It's like a wall of water on each side," one boy whispered in awe, looking at the rolling waters, then at the dry ground in the middle. "The Lord God has delivered us."

Another glanced back. "But the Egyptians will follow. See? They are already starting to drive their horses and chariots into the sea!"

"Their chariot wheels are falling off," a boy shrilled. "Some are trying to turn back, but it's too late. *Look at Moses!*" He dug his fingers into his friend's arm until the other boy cried out with pain, although he could not tear his gaze away from their leader.

They watched in awe as Moses stretched his hand out over the sea again. The waters that had parted now roiled and churned, swallowing up Egyptians, chariots, horsemen, and all the host of Pharaoh that came into the sea. But the children of Israel safely walked between the walls of water on their right and left hand and were safe.

Exodus 14

the coming of the quails

"Mother, I am so hungry." The young girl clasped her hands over her stomach.

Her mother sighed. "I know, my daughter. I am hungry, too, but there is barely anything left to eat. It is the same throughout the camp." She shook her head. "Perhaps the people who are crying out against Moses and Aaron are right. It seemed a good thing for us to leave Egypt, but if we don't find food soon, we may die of hunger in the wilderness."

The girl crept close within her mother's arms. "Why don't Moses and Aaron do something? Has God forsaken us?"

"Nay. Perhaps He is merely testing our faith. Remember how He parted the waters of the Red Sea and delivered us from Pharaoh? And how He caused the waters to return and cover our enemies? Come, child. I will see if there are a few grains of meal left, enough to make a little cake for you."

"For you, too, Mother," the girl replied. "Thank you for reminding me that God has not forgotten us." She rubbed her growling stomach. "I just wish He would send us some food!"

God had not forsaken His people. He told Moses, "I will rain bread from heaven for you. The people will go out each day and gather enough for that day. On the sixth day, they will gather twice as much. In the evening you will eat flesh and in the morning you shall be filled with bread, that you may know I am the Lord your God."

That evening the girl rushed to her mother. "Come quickly! Hundreds of quail are covering the camp. The men are catching them. We shall have food this night, just as the Lord said!"

"Praise to His name," her mother said. "He has seen our need and provided for us in the wilderness."

Soon the aroma of roasting meat spread over the encampment like a thick fog. Hungry children and adults could barely wait for it to be ready. Every person ate until he or she was filled and then lay down to sleep in peace.

The girl awakened early the next morning. She looked around, rubbed her eyes, and looked again. Heavy dew covered the ground all around the camp, making it look whiter than snow. When the dew was gone, it left tiny, frostlike round things.

"What is it, Mother?" the girl inquired.

She shook her head. "I don't know."

Some of the people said it was manna, but Moses told them, "This is the bread that the Lord promised He would give for you to eat. You are to gather enough for every person in your tent."

The people did so, and the strangest thing happened. Those who gathered much did not have any left over. Those who needed and gathered less had plenty!

"Do not try to keep any until morning," Moses warned.

A few people disobeyed, but the next day the manna had rotted!

Every morning God sent fresh manna, enough for that day. On the sixth day, He sent enough so the people could bake for the Sabbath, when no manna would come. Unlike the other days, what was collected and held over for the Sabbath meals remained fresh.

"God is so good to us," the girl told her mother. "I am sorry we thought He might have forsaken us."

"So am I." The woman paused in her work to smile at her daughter and then went back to preparing manna for them to eat on the Sabbath.

Exodus 16

Day after weary day, the children of Israel journeyed from the wilderness of Sin, just as the Lord had commanded. It was a long, hard trek. Children fretted and became bored with placing one sandaled foot after the other and following their parents. Every day was a repeat of the day before—and the day before that. It was little better for their parents. The high enthusiasm that had sustained them earlier in their travels, the relief and joy over being free from bondage, had all too quickly faded. More and more they murmured against Moses and complained that God had forsaken them.

"I wish we would get where we are going," a disgruntled boy burst out one afternoon when the sun beat down on the caravan.

"Wherever that is," one of his cousins retorted. "I'm beginning to wonder if there really is a Promised Land or if Moses and Aaron are lost."

"Oh, there's a Promised Land," another put in. "We just won't reach it if we don't find water soon. I'm so thirsty I could drink the Nile River dry!"

The first boy made a gagging sound. "Not me. The water is too dirty." He licked his dry, cracked lips and sighed. "We are going to pitch our tents in Rephidim. There is sure to be water there."

"There had better be!" his cousin grimly said. "The people are ready to stone Moses for bringing us here."

"A lot of good that would do," the other replied. "Without Moses, we will never get out of this wilderness. We probably couldn't even find our way back to Egypt."

His sober words brought silence to the group. The boys knew only too well that their cousin had spoken the truth.

When they reached Rephidim and pitched their tents, the boys quickened their pace, eager to find water.

There was none.

A wave of protest arose from the thirsty multitude. "Give us water, Moses, that we may drink," the people commanded. "What is this? Have you brought us out of Egypt to kill our children and our cattle with thirst?" Their shouts grew louder and more menacing as more and more people took up the cry.

The cousins looked at one another. If the Lord didn't intervene—and soon—something terrible would surely happen to Moses.

Moses knew the mood of those he had been called to lead out of Egypt and to the Promised Land even better than the cousins did. "Why do you quarrel with me?" he demanded. "Why do you tempt the Lord?" Yet the crowd continued to complain bitterly. Then Moses cried out to the Lord, saying, "What shall I do? The people are ready to stone me."

"Take some of the elders and walk ahead of the people. Take the rod with which you smote the River Nile; take it in your hand and go. I will stand before you upon the rock of Horeb. When you smite the rock, water will come forth so the people may drink."

Moses did what the Lord commanded. He lifted up his rod and struck the rock of Horeb with a powerful blow. *Crack!* The sound echoed throughout the encampment. A moment later, pure, clean water gushed from the rock with a great roar. People rushed forward to quench their thirst, thanking the same God they had railed against such a short time before. But Moses named the place Massah ("temptation, testing") and Meribah ("quarreling") because of what happened there.

Exodus 17; Numbers 20

moses and the Lord

Three months after the children of Israel had left Egypt, they reached the wilderness of Sinai. Weary from their travels, they set up their tents at the foot of the mountain that rose high above the Sinai desert.

One day Moses left the people and went up the mountain.

"Where is he going? Is he going to leave us here and not be our leader?" a little girl asked her older sister.

The sister shook her head. "No. God has called to Moses from the mountain and told him to come to Him."

"Why did God do that?" the child wanted to know.

"I don't know," her sister admitted, "but Father says God wishes to speak with Moses and that Moses will tell us what the voice of the Lord says when he comes down from the mountain."

"Oh." Satisfied, the younger girl ran off to find her mother.

When Moses returned from talking with God, his face shone like sunlight on a sparkling river. "I have good tidings," he joyously told the people. "The Lord will come to the top of Mount Sinai in a thick cloud. He told me that when you hear Him speak with me, you will believe me. Today and tomorrow I am to bless and sanctify you. You are to wash your clothes and be ready, for on the third day, the Lord will come down, as He has promised."

He raised his hand to still the murmur that raced through the crowd. "You must be careful. Do not go up to the mountain or even touch it. It will not be safe for you to do so until after the trumpet blows a long sound."

"Isn't it exciting?" the older sister exclaimed to her younger sister. "God Himself is going to come to the mountain!" She scrubbed away at a piece of clothing until it was as clean as she could make it. "We are to hear God's voice!"

"What does God look like? Will we be able to see Him?" her sister wondered.

The older sister looked shocked. "Oh, no! The cloud in which God will stand will be far too thick."

On the morning of the third day, thunder and lightning filled the sky. A thick cloud came over the mountain, followed by a loud trumpet call, so strong that all the people in the camp trembled. Moses led the people to the foot of Mount Sinai to meet with God. Great clouds of smoke billowed up as the Lord descended. The mountain quaked. The trumpet blew louder and louder. Moses spoke, and the voice of God answered, telling him to come to the top of the mountain.

When Moses returned, he warned the people again not to try to climb the mountain to see God. Only Aaron was to go with Moses.

"Why doesn't God want us to see Him?" the young girl asked her sister.

The older girl looked solemn. "Father and Mother say God is too holy for us to see." She brightened. "We can always remember that we heard His voice, though."

The people did remember—for a time. Yet after many days passed and Moses did not come back to the camp at the foot of Mount Sinai, they began to murmur and complain again.

Exodus 19–20, 34

a golden calf

"Where is Moses?"

The unanswered question spread throughout the encampment at the foot of Mount Sinai like warm honey on freshly baked bread. To those who awaited their leader's coming, it seemed as if Moses had been gone forever. Even though the children of Israel had trembled at the fearsome sights and sounds when the Lord came to the mountain, now they whispered to one another, "Perhaps a wild beast has devoured him, or the Lord has carried Moses away in a cloud of smoke."

"Is Moses dead?" a small boy asked his mother.

The mother wrapped her son in her shawl and said, "No one knows."

"What will we do if he doesn't come back? Will we die, too?" the child wailed.

She shook her head. "Aaron or one of the elders will lead us." She held him close. "Do not fret. Surely God has not brought us to this place to die." She took a deep, troubled breath. "I just wish Moses would return. There is much talk among the people. . . ." Her voice trailed off.

In the following days the rumbling of discontent spread throughout the multitude. Finally a great crowd approached Aaron. "Make us gods that will go before us. As for this Moses, the man who brought us out of the land of Egypt, we know not what has become of him."

Aaron listened to their pleas and said, "Break off the golden earrings that are in the ears of your wives, of your sons, and of your daughters. Bring them to me."

The people did what he commanded. They brought the golden earrings and laid them before Aaron. When he had a goodly pile, he took tools and fashioned them into an idol, a molten calf. He built an altar before the golden calf. "Tomorrow there will be a festival to the Lord," he proclaimed. The next day the people rose early. They sacrificed burnt offerings and brought peace offerings. They sat down, ate and drank, and then leaped up to dance wildly before the golden calf.

"Why are they dancing?" the small boy whispered.

"Shhh," his mother said. "Come. We will go into our tent away from all this."

Up on the mountain, God told Moses, "Get down to the people. They have turned from the way I commanded and made an idol in the shape of a calf. Leave Me alone so I may destroy them for their wickedness and make of you a great nation."

Moses pleaded, "You brought them out of Egypt with great power and a mighty hand. If You destroy them, the Egyptians will say that You led them away only to kill them."

The Lord relented and did not bring disaster on the people.

Moses hastened down the mountain. His anger grew with

every step. When he saw the calf and the people dancing before it, he broke the tablets of stone on which God had written laws for the people. He burned them in the fire and ground them to powder. He scattered it on the water and made the people drink it.

Aaron tried to excuse himself for what he and the people had done, but they did not escape punishment. The Lord sent a plague. Many died, but the mother, son, and all who did not worship the golden calf were spared.

Exodus 32

moses sends out spies

"Did you hear the news?" a Hebrew boy, panting with excitement, asked a group of friends. "We are getting close to the land of Canaan. Moses says God is going to give it to us, and Moses is going to send spies into the land."

"How do you know?" his friends chorused.

"I heard it with my own ears." Longing stole into his face. "How I wish I could go! I would—"

"They will not let any of us go," a boy interrupted. He flexed a muscled arm. "Even though we are strong from hard work, our lack of years is against us."

A mutter of agreement rippled through the group before the first boy said, "A man from each tribe is to go, one of the leaders."

Several boys scowled. "If I could find a way to hide and not be discovered, I would go with them," one declared.

"You had better not try," another advised. "Not only would you be found out and sent back, but it would go hard with you for daring such a thing."

"I know." His sigh sounded as if it came all the way from his dusty bare toes in his trail-worn sandals. He brightened. "At least we can be the first to see the men when they return! Every day we will watch and wait, taking turns between our camp duties."

"That's a good idea," the others readily agreed. "I hope they aren't gone too long. I can hardly wait to learn what they find out!"

When the twelve men were ready to go, Moses gave them strict orders. "Travel south and up into the mountain. See if the land is bad or good, fat or lean. Learn about the cities where the people dwell, whether in tents or strongholds. Take notice whether the people are strong or weak, few or many, and if there is wood in the land. Be of good courage and bring back some of the fruit that grows there."

The spies did as they were commanded. They found ripe grapes, pomegranates, and figs. For forty days they searched out the land, and then they returned to their people.

The boy on duty raced through the camp, crying, "Joshua and Caleb and the others are coming!" Everyone hurried to hear what the spies had found out.

"It is a land that flows with milk and honey," they said, "but those who inhabit it are strong. The cities are walled and great."

Disappointed cries rose from the crowd. After their long, hard journey, such a place sounded like the garden in which God had placed the first man and woman.

"Let us go up at once and possess it," Caleb urged. "We are well able to overcome."

"Nay," others protested. "They are stronger than we. There are giants so large that we seemed like grasshoppers compared to them!"

The disillusioned people wept and again accused Moses and Aaron of bringing them to the wilderness to die. They decided to appoint a captain and return to Egypt!

God's patience with those who had seen His miracles and continued to doubt Him ended. No one over twenty years of age except Joshua and Caleb would be allowed to enter and possess the Promised Land. For forty years, the children would be shepherds in the wilderness, and then they would inherit the land flowing with milk and honey. The boys would be included, but not until they were men.

Numbers 13–14

balaam and his talking donkey

God's sacred book, the Bible, occasionally contains true humor ranging from Old Testament foibles to the exaggerated illustrations used by Christ Himself. (Envision a camel passing through the eye of a needle!)

Here is Balaam, a soothsayer from Mesopotamia, riding his donkey to visit King Balak of Moab. King Balak has a problem: The Israelites, wandering from Egypt to the Promised Land, have arrived at the Jordan River, and Balak sees them as a threat to his kingdom. They are God's chosen people and have already conquered entire armies. Balak does not want to fight them; he knows the Israelites are too strong. Yet if they remain in his territory, Balak fears they will consume everything in sight. They must be driven away.

Balak has a solution: Summon Balaam and have this Gentile prophet place a curse on the Israelites. He does so and promises Balaam a handsome reward.

Balaam wrestles with this proposal. When the Lord tells him plainly that the Israelites have God's own blessing, Balaam dutifully refuses Balak's request. "How can I curse what the Lord has blessed?" he reasons. Balak persists, and God permits Balaam to go to the king. "But do only what I tell you to do," the Lord commands. The Lord wants to impress upon Balaam His unhappiness with Balak's proposal and the importance of Balaam's strict obedience in this situation. The fact that God chooses to do this is memorable.

On the way to Moab, Balaam receives a sequence of rude surprises by his donkey. First, the animal suddenly leaves the road and carries him into a field. Later, the donkey brushes against a stone wall, scraping Balaam's foot. Then the donkey lies down and refuses to move. Each time, Balaam angrily beats the poor creature. What Balaam has failed to see is that on each occasion, the donkey has been halted by an angel with a sword. Finally Balaam gets the greatest surprise of all: The donkey looks at him and speaks!

"Why are you beating me?" asks the donkey.

"Because you embarrassed me," rebukes the astonished rider. "If I had a sword, I would kill you."

"Have I ever acted this way before?" challenges the donkey.

Upon reflection, Balaam has to admit, "No."

While the distracted diviner is discoursing with his donkey in what is perhaps the most hilarious scene in the entire Bible, the Lord reveals the angel to him. The awestruck traveler bows to his knees, apologizes for beating his frightened donkey, and offers to return home, if God so desires. The angel instructs Balaam to proceed to Moab but reminds him to say exactly what the Lord tells him to say.

Balaam follows God's bidding and instead of cursing the Israelites, he blesses them three times, to King Balak's chagrin. The king sends Balaam away, thinking him a fool for squandering the chance to earn a king's reward. But Balaam corrects him: "Even if you offered me a house full of money, I could not disobey the Lord." These are bold words to say to an angry king! But in the wake of his experience with the donkey, Balaam understands very clearly who is the true King.

Numbers 22–24

"You're the one who will lead our people into God's Promised Land."

Those words, spoken by the aging Moses, must have thrilled Joshua's heart—and given him much trepidation. There were strong nations to conquer once the Hebrews crossed the Jordan River. "Do not be afraid," Moses told him. "God Himself will lead you. He will not abandon you."

Israel reached the Jordan near Jericho at flood time. A crossing seemed impossible. But God told Joshua He would perform a miracle to display the fact that God's blessings were with him. And sure enough, when the priests carrying the ark of God's covenant waded into the swollen waters, the river stopped flowing! The people were able to go across the dry river bottom.

One day near Jericho, Joshua encountered an angel with a sword. "Are you friend or foe?" Joshua asked, thinking the angel was human.

"Neither," the angel replied. "I am captain of the Lord's army."

Joshua bowed low to the angel, who commanded him to take off his sandals. "You're standing on holy ground," the angel said.

Joshua may be remembered best for the capture of Jericho. It was a well-guarded city, but the Lord told Joshua it was his for the taking. God's tactic was simple but strange. The Israelite army, led by priests carrying the ark of the covenant, was to march around the city for six days. On the seventh day, the priests were to blow trumpets while soldiers marched around the city seven times. Then as the trumpets sounded one extended note, the soldiers were to shout, and the walls of Jericho would collapse!

In this way Jericho was leveled and its inhabitants annihilated. Joshua placed the Lord's curse on anyone who might try to rebuild the city.

At long last the Israelites settled in Canaan, the Promised Land. Joshua ruled wisely, and the Lord sent miracles to help Joshua's army subdue their enemies. Joshua divided the land among the Israelites and renewed their covenant with the Lord. He gave his people a choice: Worship the one true God and be blessed, or keep worthless idols and suffer punishment. "As for my household," said Joshua, "we will serve the Lord."

Deuteronomy 31:1–8; 34:5–9; Joshua

rahab, harlot of jericho

Rahab, harlot and innkeeper, stared into the faces of the two strangers who had taken lodging in her house. What manner of men were they, these bold Israelites who dared enter Jericho? As she spoke with them, the gossip that had raced through the streets of Jericho and into every house kept time with their story. A strange and unexplainable feeling came, an assurance that all she had heard of the protecting hand of the Lord who watched over His chosen people was true. Yet what had she to do with the matter? The men had obviously come to spy out the land, with full intentions of making it their own. Even now one of the king's men would be seeking the Israelites.

Rahab scarcely believed her own ears when she whispered, "Come!" Heart beating wildly, she led them to the roof of the house. She hid them under stalks of flax, laid in order on the roof. "Do not make a sound, or you will surely be discovered," she ordered them. "If you are, you bring death not only to yourselves, but to all of the house of Rahab." She slipped away.

A loud pounding on the door sent blood hurrying through her veins. She flung it open. "What do you want?" she demanded of the king's guard.

"In the name of the king, bring forth the men that are come to thee," came the reply. "It has been told to the king of Jericho they are children of Israel, come to search out the country."

Rahab didn't betray herself by even the blink of an eyelash. "There came men to me, but I wist not whence they were; it came to pass that the men went out, about the time of the shutting of the gate when darkness fell. Pursue them quickly; for ye shall overtake them."

The king's men eyed her suspiciously; Rahab's steady glance did not waver. She stood in the doorway until she was certain they had gone, then waited a time to make sure none lurked behind to see if she spoke the truth.

When all grew still, Rahab went back to the roof. She told the spies, "I know the Lord hath given you the land. Your terror is fallen upon us, and all the inhabitants of the land faint because of you. When we heard how the Lord dried up the water of the Red Sea for you when you came out of Egypt, our hearts did melt, neither did there remain any more courage in any man, because of you: for the Lord your God is God in heaven above, and in earth beneath." She paused, hands clenched and wet with sweat.

"I pray you, swear unto me by the Lord, since I have showed you kindness, that you will also show kindness unto my father's house, and give me a true token. . .save alive my father, and my mother, and my brethren, and my sisters, and all that they have, and deliver our lives from death."

The Israelites exchanged glances. They promised Rahab if she kept silent about the whole business, when the Lord gave them the land, they would deal kindly and truly with her.

Great relief filled her. "Come." She took them to the window and let them down by a cord, for her house was upon the town wall, but not before they asked her to tie a line of scarlet thread in the same window and bring her family and all their household inside the inn. Whosoever went outside would die. All who remained inside the house with the scarlet thread would be spared.

Rahab did as she was commanded. When the walls of

Jericho fell before Joshua and his men, only Rahab and those with her in the house did not perish. The two young spies she had saved took her and her kindred outside the camp of Israel. Her heart burned within her. One act of kindness had brought mercy for those she loved.

The genealogy of Christ given in Matthew 1 lists Rahab as the mother of Boaz, great-grandfather of King David. If this is she who saved Joshua's men, it seems likely Rahab turned from her wickedness and sought forgiveness from the Lord she recognized as God of heaven and earth.

Joshua 2, 6

the storming of jericho

Forty long years of hardship and wandering in the wilderness crept by. One by one, all the men of military age who came out of Egypt died and were buried in the desert. The time had come for their sons to inherit the land God had vowed their fathers would not see. Only Caleb and Joshua were left of their generation to enter the land flowing with milk and honey.

The day after the Israelites celebrated the Passover, the manna from heaven stopped coming. That day they ate some of the produce of the land: unleavened bread and roasted grain. There was no longer need for the manna.

God had put Joshua in charge after Moses died, and he led the people on the journey they had begun so long ago. At last they reached Jericho.

When Joshua came near the city, he looked up and saw a man with drawn sword in front of him. "Are you for us or for our enemies?" Joshua inquired.

"Neither. I now come as commander of the army of the Lord," the man replied.

Joshua fell to the ground before him. "What message does my Lord have for me, His servant?"

"Take off your shoes. The place where you stand is holy."

Joshua quickly removed his sandals as he had been directed.

"See," the Lord said, "I have given you Jericho and the king and all his mighty fighting men." He went on to tell Joshua what he must do to enter the city closed against the Israelites, a city so walled and secure that no one could leave or enter.

"Take all your armed men and march around the city once. Do this every day for six days. Seven priests are to bear seven trumpets before the ark [the sacred chest representing to the Hebrews the presence of God among them]. On the seventh day, you are to march around the city seven times, with the priests blowing on the trumpets. When they make a long blast, all the people must shout with a great shout. The wall of the city shall fall down flat, and every man shall go straight inside the city."

"I don't understand," a young maiden said to her brother, when the people learned what God had ordered them to do. She pointed to the massive wall that surrounded Jericho. "How can just walking around a city blowing on trumpets and shouting make those walls fall down?"

"If God says it will happen, it will happen," he told her. "Don't you remember the tales of how He parted the waters and brought water from a rock in the wilderness? Is it any harder to set walls tumbling than to feed us with manna?"

"N—no," she admitted.

"It will be a sight to behold," he said. "Now we must speak no more. Joshua has commanded silence until he gives the order for us to shout on the seventh day."

For six days the people watched and obeyed God's command, given by Joshua. On the seventh, they arose knowing this would be the day their ancestors had waited for ever since being taken into captivity in Egypt. Children and adults alike watched in awe as the marchers completed their final round.

The mighty trumpet blast sounded. It echoed against the city walls and bounced back to the waiting Israelites. Joshua gave the signal. The people's voices rose in a single, mighty shout.

The next instant, the walls of Jericho crumbled. God had kept His promise.

Joshua 6

a charge to the people

When the walls of Jericho fell in ruins, Joshua warned, "If you take things from the city, it will bring destruction on us. All the silver and gold, bronze and iron are sacred to the Lord and must go into His treasury."

Some of the people were greedy. They broke the covenant with the Lord, stole forbidden items, and hid them with their own possessions. Because they disobeyed, God told Joshua, "I will not be with you any longer unless you destroy those forbidden things stolen by the people." Joshua found them and did as the Lord commanded.

Joshua found that ruling over the Israelites wasn't any easier than it had been for Moses. No matter how often the Lord blessed them and helped them defeat their enemies, many were never satisfied.

A day like no other came during war with the Amorites. Battle sounds drifted back to the camp, striking fear into the hearts of those who waited.

"Our men are strong," a boy told his brother. "And Joshua goes in the name of the Lord."

"The Amorites are strong, too." His brother shaded his eyes and looked into the heavens. "Why is the sun still in the middle of the sky at this hour?"

His brother tilted his head back. "It should not be there. Let's ask Father."

The boys discovered him in the midst of a group of pointing, babbling men. "The sun, Father. It is—"

"I know." He brushed them aside. "It should be setting but hangs as if fixed in the sky. Never in the history of time has such a thing happened!"

"What does it mean?" the boys wanted to know.

"It surely is a sign from God," their father said.

Hours fled by. When time for darkness came, the sun remained in the same position. The moon did not rise. At last the brothers grew so tired that their weary eyelids drooped. The boys stumbled back to their sleeping mats. When they awakened early the next morning, the sun had not budged from where it had stopped in the middle of the sky the day before!

"How long will it be day?" the brothers asked their father.

He shook his head. "I cannot say. It is reported that Joshua asked God to make the sun stand still so we could be victorious over the Amorites. Surely the Lord is fighting for us."

The sun delayed going down for a whole day. Joshua and his men returned, having driven the Amorites away.

Many years passed. Joshua knew he would soon die. He called all Israel together and told the people what God would have them hear. He warned that if they turned from the Lord and mingled with the survivors of the enemy nations God had helped them overcome, He would no longer be with them.

Then Joshua issued a challenge that would ring down through the ages: "If it seems evil to serve the Lord, choose you this day whom you will serve; whether the gods which your fathers served on the other side of the flood, or the gods of the Amorites, in whose land you dwell." Every child old enough to understand never forgot Joshua's face when he proclaimed, "As for me and my house, we will serve the Lord."

Inspired by their leader's words, the people cried, "The Lord our God will we serve, and His voice will we obey." Joshua wrote these words in the book of the law of God, that they might be recorded forever.

Joshua 24

Deborah, prophetess and judge of Israel, dwelled beneath her palm tree between Ramah and Bethel. The children of Israel came to her for judgments in disputes they either could not or would not settle on their own. Sometimes Lapidoth, her husband, felt they taxed his wife beyond measure, yet he took great pride in the wisdom of her decisions. Did not all who knew Deborah love and respect her for the high position to which Jehovah had called her?

Not all of Deborah's troubles came from those she served. The Lord had also burdened her concerning her people. War with Sisera, captain of King Jabin's army, loomed as inevitable. Anticipation of the forthcoming battle lay on Deborah's heart like a heavy stone.

One day she called Barak, son of Abinoam from Kedesh-naphtali, and demanded, "Has the Lord God of Israel not commanded us to go toward Mount Tabor, taking ten thousand men of the children of Naphtali and Zebulun? Jehovah Himself has promised to draw Sisera with his chariots and multitude to the river Kishon and deliver him into our hand."

Barak, resembling the thunderbolt and lightning for which he had been named, flung his head back. "If you will go with me, I will go. If you will not, then I will not go."

Deborah faced him squarely. A dozen thoughts chased through her active brain. A woman in battle, leading against the foe? Such a thing had never been heard of. What would those she judged think of her? *Why not?* she silently asked herself. Had not God called her first as a prophetess, then as a judge? "I will go, notwithstanding the journey you take shall not be for your honor. The Lord shall sell Sisera into the hand of a woman."

Barak agreed, and Deborah arose straightway and went with him to Kedesh, where Zebulun and Naphtali awaited them in answer to Barak's call. Ten thousand men responded and accompanied Barak and Deborah.

On the morning of the battle, Deborah said to Barak, "Up, for this is the day in which the Lord has delivered Sisera into your hand."

When Sisera heard that Barak had gone up to Mount Tabor, he gathered together his nine hundred chariots of iron and a multitude of warriors. A terrible battle ensued, but the Lord discomfited Sisera, his chariots, and all his host. When the battle ended, not an enemy remained alive.

Deborah and Barak joined in a song of praise, thanking God for delivering the foe into their hands. They spoke of how God sent a mother in Israel to defeat those who had chosen new gods. They named those who had joined Deborah and Barak in the fray: the princes of Issachar; kings who came and fought without gain of money. They sang, "They fought from heaven; the stars in their courses fought against Sisera."

At last, the ceaseless pounding in Deborah's soul stilled. The land had rest for forty years. The name of Deborah took its place in history as one who first judged, then led her people both wisely and well.

Judges 4–5

gideon's small army

He was not a man to be trifled with, as many a foe discovered. Happily, Gideon was on the side of the Israelites.

During the time of the judges, God let Israel be subjugated by Midian, and for seven years the children of Israel were impoverished victims of their conquerors.

After they had suffered long enough, the Lord spoke to Gideon. This poor Israelite from Ophrah was trying to hoard a supply of wheat from his captors, but God had more important work for him to do. God told Gideon, "You will save Israel from the hand of the Midianites."

Gideon was afraid—not only of the assignment, but of his encounter with God. His tribe was weak, Gideon protested, and he was the lowest member of his own family. The Lord responded by bringing the Spirit upon Gideon.

Thus empowered, Gideon sounded a trumpet and sent messengers to gather an army. Thirty-two thousand men initially joined him. "This is too many," God told him. If Israel won the victory with such a large army, the people would assume credit for themselves and deny the power of God. So Gideon invited those who were afraid of fighting to turn back. This left him with ten thousand soldiers.

"Still too many," the Lord said—doubtless stirring Gideon's uneasiness. To reduce the number of soldiers further, God told Gideon to send the soldiers to the water's edge to drink. The ones who lapped the water as a dog would drink were to be separated from those who knelt to drink the water cupped in their hands. Three hundred men lapped to drink. God told Gideon to discharge all the others. "I will deliver the Midianites into your hands."

The Midianites camped in the valley were as thick as locusts; their camels were as numerous as sand on the seashore. Gideon naturally was timid, so the Lord told him to slip into the Midianite camp at night and promised to show him a sign there for reassurance. When Gideon crept near the Midianite camp, he heard two men talking. One was relating a dream he'd had of a bread loaf tumbling into camp and flattening one of the tents. His friend interpreted the dream: "The bread loaf is the sword of the Israelite Gideon. God will deliver the whole Midianite camp into his hands!" Gideon knew his mission was secure.

Gideon and his men took trumpets, jars, and torches and surrounded the Midianite camp. When signaled, they sounded the horns, smashed the jars, and waved the torches. The sudden clamor on all sides wakened the Midianites to a scene of total confusion. In their rush to escape, they mistakenly attacked and killed many of their own comrades.

Other Israelites were summoned and completely routed the Midianites. As Gideon and his three hundred commandos chased the Midianite kings across the Jordan River, they wearily stopped at the towns of Succoth and Penuel and requested food, but the leaders of both towns refused to help them. Gideon angrily warned that when he returned with the two kings in tow, the insolent town leaders would be punished severely. He was as good as his word. Succoth and Penuel were punished, and the captured kings of Midian were put to death.

The grateful Israelites wanted Gideon and his descendants to be their rulers. But Gideon responded, "The Lord will rule over you."

Gideon's story ends on the unhappy note of forgetfulness and idolatry. In the aftermath of his unprecedented victory, Gideon collected the gold earrings captured from the Midianites. They were melted and cast into an idol, which Gideon took to his hometown of Ophrah. Then, as is the pattern in the book of the Judges, Israel forgot God and gathered in Ophrah to worship Gideon's idol.

Judges 6–8

manoah's wife, mother of samson

A certain man named Manoah, whose wife was barren, lived in the midst of the children of Israel, who again did evil in the sight of the Lord and were delivered into the hand of the Philistines for forty years.

One day an angel of the Lord appeared unto the woman and said unto her, "Behold, now thou art barren and bearest not: but thou shalt conceive and bear a son. Now therefore beware, I pray thee, and drink not wine nor strong drink, and eat not any unclean thing: For, lo, thou shalt conceive, and bear a son; and no razor shall come on his head: for the child shall be a Nazarite unto God from the womb: and he shall begin to deliver Israel out of the hand of the Philistines."

Manoah's wife rejoiced greatly and ran to tell her husband. "A man of God came unto me, and his countenance was like the countenance of an angel of God, very terrible. But I asked him not whence he was, neither told he me his name." She faithfully related the rest of the angel's message.

Manoah, much impressed, entreated the Lord, asking for the man of God to come again and teach them what they should do for the child who would be born. God heard the prayer. The angel came to the woman in the field. She made haste and brought Manoah to him. The angel repeated the instructions he had given earlier but refused to eat bread with them. Manoah took a young goat and made an offering. When the flame rose, the angel of the Lord ascended in the flame of the altar. Manoah and his wife looked on it and fell on their faces to the ground.

"We shall surely die," Manoah wailed. "We have seen God."

His wife reminded him God would not have showed them all those things if He planned to kill them. She kept that hope in her heart and one day bore a son. "He shall be called Samson, which means 'like the sun,' " she told her husband.

The child grew, and the Lord blessed him. When Samson became a young man, a daughter of the Philistines found favor in his eyes. His mother's heart quailed within her. She and Manoah protested, "Is there not a woman among the daughters of thy brethren, or among all my people, that thou goest to take a wife of the uncircumcised Philistines?"

Samson insisted they get her for him, for she pleased him well. Sad-hearted, his mother traveled with her husband and son to the vineyards of Timnath. There a young lion roared against Samson. The Spirit of the Lord came so mightily upon the young man that he killed the lion—but he did not tell his father or mother. Still, they realized their son had been set apart before his birth to do great things.

Samson's mother kept her counsel. The father made a contract with the woman their son desired, and Samson held a great feast. Strong, untamed, uncut hair hanging over his mighty shoulders, he sent a thrill of pride through his mother, although her woman's heart feared for him because he had chosen a Philistine's daughter to wed.

Her fears proved well grounded. Men at the feast threatened to burn the bride and her father's house if she did not entice Samson to give her the answer to a riddle he had posed. If they could declare the answer in the seven days of the feast, they would receive thirty sheets and thirty changes of garments. If not, they would furnish Samson with the same.

The bride wept and teased, saying Samson did not love but hated her. He finally gave her the answer. She immediately told the men of the city. They taunted Samson until his anger kindled and he retaliated, then went up to his father's house.

Samson's mother grieved for him, even more when he went for his wife and found her father had given her to a companion Samson thought was a friend. Was it for this he had been born? Nay. In spite of doubt, she remembered the angel's words and took comfort: He shall begin to deliver Israel out of the hand of the Philistines. Perhaps everything that had happened was according to a heavenly plan and a sign that deliverance had started.

Judges 13–15

samson, foe of the philistines

Today's superheroes of sports are weaklings compared to a real hero who lived three thousand years ago. When Samson flexed his muscles, heavy cords snapped like rotten string. He once slew a thousand enemies using the jawbone of a donkey for a weapon. He uprooted the gates of the city of Gaza and carried them to the top of a distant hill. When attacked by a lion, he made no attempt to escape or tame the animal; with his bare hands he tore its jaws apart! How many of our professional football stars—or entire championship teams—do you suppose would attempt that?

Samson's feats were the work of the Lord. The Spirit of God came over him, and suddenly he was empowered with incredible strength.

Samson was a Hebrew judge during the years when God allowed the Israelites to fall captive to the Philistines. The wife of the Israelite Manoah learned from an angel of the Lord that she would give birth to a son who would rescue the Jews from their captors. When Samson was born, the Holy Spirit came upon him, and he grew to become the Philistines' terror. On one occasion he killed thirty of them. Another time he caught three hundred foxes, tied torches to their tails, and ran them through the Philistines' fields, thus causing their crops to burn. After slaughtering more Philistines, Samson went into the wilderness and lived in a cave.

At one point Samson let himself be captured and turned over to the Philistines. But when his enemies began to celebrate his capture, he snapped his bonds and massacred them.

The Philistines finally found a way to contain him. He fell in love with a woman named Delilah. The Philistine leaders offered her an enormous sum of money if she could find out the source of Samson's strength as a game. "Tie me up with seven unseasoned bow strings," he told her. "That will normalize my power." Delilah tied him up and summoned the Philistines to come for him. But when he saw them, Samson immediately broke free.

"New ropes will do it," he teased. "Tie me in ropes that have never been used."

Again she tied him, and again he broke his bonds.

Samson had long, wavy hair that had never been cut. "Weave my hair in your loom," he said, "and I'll be as weak as any other man." But again, when Delilah thought she and her conspirators had him at bay, Samson laughingly broke away.

At last he told her the true secret of his strength. "I was dedicated to God when I was born," he said, "so my hair has never been cut. My hair is the key to my strength." Soon Delilah sang him softly to sleep and cut his hair. When he awoke and tried to summon his strength, he found that the Spirit had left him. He was captured. The Philistines put out his eyes, bound him in chains, and threw him in prison where he was forced to grind their grain.

Later the inebriated Philistines were at a festival in honor of their pagan god. They called for Samson to be brought from the dungeon into their temple so they could mock him publicly. Several thousand people were gathered to taunt the once-proud Israelite. But Samson's hair had grown back. He slyly persuaded his guard to position his hands for him between the two main pillars of the temple. Then he prayed that God would strengthen him for one last mighty feat.

God answered his prayer. Samson pushed against the great pillars as hard as he could; they gave way, and the temple collapsed on the hordes of Philistine mockers—and on Samson. It is recorded that he killed more Philistines with his last act than he had killed in all his other deeds combined.

Judges 13–16

delilah, snare to samson

Delilah of Sorek listened well when the lords of the Philistines came up to her. Hatred filled their faces and spilled over into their words. "Entice the man Samson," they said. "See wherein his great strength lies, and by what means we may prevail against him. . . . We will give thee every one of us eleven hundred pieces of silver."

Delilah's eyes glistened with greed. Such a paltry task! Was not Samson already entrapped by her charms? Knowledge of her power over men made the proposition even more attractive. Eyes half-closed, she envisioned the velvets and silks, gold chains and rich jewels she would buy to enhance her perfumed body that drove men to madness.

When Samson came to her, Delilah began her campaign against the man who loved her. "Tell me," she began, "where does it come from, the strength you possess? Should one wish to afflict you, how could it be done?"

Samson caressed her smooth cheek. "If I were bound with seven green cords that were never dried, I would be as weak as any other man."

Delilah promptly reported the answer to the lords of the Philistines. They brought her the seven green cords that had not been dried. Men lay in wait inside her chamber, and when Delilah bound Samson, she cried, "The Philistines be upon thee, Samson!"

He sprang to his feet, breaking the cords as if they were single threads.

Delilah's face resembled a thundercloud. "Why do you mock me and lie to me? Tell me the truth, Samson."

This time he told her that if his enemies bound him with new ropes that had never been used, he would be weak. She bound him, called out, and grew enraged when he broke them as easily as he had the green cords. Again she asked the secret of his strength, chagrined to find the power she thought she had over him had not yet been his undoing. Images of the vast fortune she had been promised faded.

Fury burned within her. It should not be so! She bound his locks, fastened them with a pin, and watched Samson once more effortlessly free himself.

With tears and cajoling, Delilah vexed Samson until he told her all his heart. "There hath not come a razor upon my head; I have been a Nazarite unto God from my mother's womb. If I be shaven, then my strength will go from me, and I shall become weak and be like any other man."

Delilah felt torn between hope and the fear it was only another lie, but she reported to the Philistines, who brought the promised money. She made Samson sleep; a man came and shaved the luxuriant, uncut hair. This time when she cried, "The Philistines be upon thee," Samson awoke and said, "I will go out as at other times before, and shake myself." He did not know the Lord had departed from him. The Philistines took him away, leaving Delilah to gloat over her ill-gotten treasure.

No record is given of Delilah from that time forward. Historians can only speculate as to whether remorse filled her shallow, wicked soul when the Philistines put out Samson's eyes, bound him with fetters of brass, and brought him to Gaza. There he ground grain in the prison house, a beast of burden. His hair began to grow, as did his repentance.

Delilah may well have been one of the Philistine men and women who made sport of Samson and praised their gods for delivering him into their hands. If so, she died with Samson and the others when God heard Samson's prayer, "O Lord God, remember me. . .and strengthen me, I pray thee only this once, O God, that I may be avenged of the Philistines for my two eyes." Taking hold of the middle pillars that held up the house, he bowed with all the restored might given by God. The walls crashed down, slaying the scheming lords and all with them.

Judges 16

naomi, mother-in-law of ruth

"Naomi, beloved." Elimelech turned a face filled with trouble toward his wife. "We cannot tarry in Bethlehem-judah any longer." Despair darkened his eyes. "Famine in our land continues, nay, grows stronger every day. We must take our sons and journey to the country of Moab. There we shall have—"

"Moab?" His good wife stared in disbelief. "Have you gone mad, my husband?" She glanced through the open doorway to where Mahlon and Chilion sat just out of hearing. "Where among the Moabites will our sons find proper wives?" Fear blanched her face and crept into her eyes. "Elimelech, this thing cannot be. Surely we must remain in our own country. Moab is filled with those who worship strange gods."

"There is food in Moab," her husband reminded. "To stay here is to starve." His gaze softened. "I like this journey no more than you, Naomi."

She said no more, but her mother's heart protested every mile of the way from Bethlehem-judah to the country of Moab, where they must sojourn. Heavy of spirit, she prayed the famine would end and they might return home. Instead, they were forced to continue in a strange land, living among those who worshiped heathen gods.

During their stay, Elimelech died, leaving Naomi bereft and alone with her two sons. Her worst fears came to pass when Mahlon and Chilion took wives of the women of Moab. Although Ruth and Orpah were comely, they were of a different faith, which sorely grieved Naomi.

Ten years later, Mahlon and Chilion also died. Naomi rocked with grief. Why had Jehovah taken first her husband, then sons? Now only the two daughters-in-law remained. What should she do? Word had come that the Lord had visited His people in the land of Judah and ended the famine. Her heart yearned within her. Oh, to return to her own country. Even the thought of it cheered her sad heart. Naomi made her choice. No longer would she dwell among those who worshiped false gods and bowed down to images of wood and stone.

The day of departure came. Although she had learned to love Orpah and Ruth, Naomi well knew the young women would surely wish to marry. Better for them to remain in the land of Moab and find husbands among their own people.

Naomi told them, "Go, return each to her mother's house. The Lord deal kindly with you, as you have dealt with the dead, and with me. The Lord grant that you may find rest, each of you in the house of her husband." She kissed them.

Orpah and Ruth lifted up their voices and wept, saying, "Surely we will return with you unto your people."

Naomi shook her head. She told them they must stay. She had no husband, no more sons to offer as husbands for Orpah and Ruth. Even if she were to marry and bear sons, there would be far too many years before they grew into manhood.

Tears fell, but Orpah at last accepted the parting. She kissed Naomi. Still weeping, she went back to her people and her gods. Ruth remained behind, cleaving to the mother-in-law she loved more than life itself. Naomi could deny her no more. Together they started up the dusty road to Bethlehem.

Ruth 1–4

ruth, moabite girl

"I have no son to be your husband," Naomi repeated to her tearful Moabite daughters-in-law.

Ruth scarcely heard her. Now that her husband lay in the grave, only Naomi remained to remind her of the happy years they had shared. She grew aware when Orpah kissed the older woman and started back to her mother's house, as Naomi had told them to do. A wave of pain washed over her. She could not—would not—let her mother-in-law go without her.

Ruth fell to her knees before Naomi. She flung her arms around the other's legs and pleaded, "Entreat me not to leave you, or to return from following after you. For where you go, I will go; and where you lodge, I will lodge: Your people shall be my people, and your God my God.

"Where you die, will I die, and there will I be buried. The Lord do so to me, and more also, if anything but death part you and me."

In the silence that fell, Ruth held her breath, asking the God of her husband to soften her mother-in-law's heart. Gradually the stiffness of Naomi's body melted. With great joy, Ruth caught the words she had so longed to hear. "Arise, my child. We shall go to Bethlehem-judah together."

They spoke no more of Ruth's impassioned plea, and when they reached Bethlehem at the beginning of the barley harvest, Naomi told those who met them, "Call me not Naomi, but Mara, for the Almighty has dealt very bitterly with me. I went out full, and the Lord has brought me home again empty."

Ruth begged to go into the fields and glean ears of corn that they might have food. She came to land belonging to Boaz, a mighty man of wealth and a kinsman of Elimelech. Ruth heard words of praise for Boaz from many and counted herself fortunate to follow the reapers in his fields. She also secretly rejoiced when he sought her out.

"Daughter, go not to glean in another field. . .abide here by my maidens. I have charged the young men not to touch you. Drink of the vessels they have drawn when you thirst."

Ruth fell to the ground. "Why have I found grace in your eyes, that you should take knowledge of me, a stranger?"

Boaz told her he knew all she had done for her mother-in-law, that she had left her own father, mother, and native land to come to a strange country. Ruth's heart stirred within her, the first time since the death of her husband. The comfort he offered showed she had found favor in his sight. She happily worked, not knowing Boaz had commanded his reapers to leave handfuls for her to glean.

Day after day Ruth gleaned in the fields—first barley, then wheat. Day after day she learned to admire Boaz more. When Naomi instructed her to wash and anoint herself and steal into the threshing floor of Boaz while he lay sleeping, then uncover his feet and lie at them, she tremblingly obeyed. Boaz awakened to find her there. He told her to tarry the night, and if the one who was a nearer kinsman than he would not take her as his wife, then he would do this thing.

All night Ruth lay sleepless, hoping the other man would refuse her. To her great joy, that kinsman drew off his shoe and sold all that belonged to Elimelech, Mahlon, and Chilion to Boaz. Boaz proclaimed to the necessary witnesses that Ruth would be his wife.

On the day of the marriage feast, Ruth remembered her vow to Naomi and silently repeated it in her heart, only this time to her husband. She would truly make his home, his people, his God, her own. Happiness filled her. It increased when the Lord blessed her and Boaz with a son. Naomi took the child, laid him in her lap, and cared for him. Ruth praised the God of Israel she had come to know and called her son Obed, which means "worshiping God."

Ruth 1–4

---

boaz, kinsman redeemer

Boaz was a wealthy man in Bethlehem during the time of the Old Testament judges. His romance and marriage to the Moabite widow Ruth is a heartwarming story of how God cares for His people in seemingly circuitous ways.

It did not take long for Boaz to notice the young stranger in his field gathering bits of grain left by his reapers. He knew this was Ruth, the foreign woman who had won the admiration of the Israelites because of her steadfast devotion in caring for her mother-in-law, Naomi, for whom she was gathering the remnants of grain.

Naomi was a Jewish woman who, with her husband, Elimelech, and their sons, had been forced out of Bethlehem by famine. They settled in the land of Moab. There Elimelech—who was a relative of Boaz—died, as did his two sons. When Naomi determined to return to her native Bethlehem, Ruth, one of her widowed daughters-in-law, vowed to come and care for her. Ruth disagreed with Naomi's reasoning that Ruth would fare better by remaining in her own land. "Wherever you go, I will go," said Ruth. "Wherever you live, I will live. Your people will be my people, and your God will be my God."

And so the two women returned to Bethlehem where Boaz not only allowed Ruth to pick up the leftover grain, but took her under his wing, as well. He invited her to eat with him and privately instructed his workers to make sure there was plenty of grain for her to gather.

It occurred to Naomi that Boaz and Ruth would be a likely, godly match. She conspired to make Ruth the focus of Boaz's attention, and a mutual interest evolved between Boaz and Ruth.

Then Boaz found a novel way to secure their union. There was one man in Bethlehem who was a closer relative of Elimelech than was Boaz. By law this man had the right to buy from Naomi the land that had belonged to her husband. So Boaz arranged a meeting with the man. Ten elders of the town were present as witnesses. Boaz proposed that if the man wanted to buy the land, he should do so; otherwise, Boaz would buy it.

"Of course I will buy it," the relative replied.

But Boaz pointed out that if the relative acquired the land, he also was obligated to marry Ruth. Their children would inherit the land, and thus the land would legally remain in the family of Ruth's dead husband, Mahlon, Elimelech's son. This the relative could not do, because it would create complications involving other property he owned. Boaz, he decided, could buy the land—and marry Ruth!

So the faithful Ruth and her long-suffering mother-in-law were well provided for. Boaz and Ruth had a son and named him Obed. Obed was the father of Jesse, the father of King David.

Ruth

Hannah, wife of Elkanah, mourned. She knew she had her husband's best love. He had given her a worthy portion of the yearly sacrifice, far more than that bestowed on his second wife, Peninnah, or to all her sons and daughters. If only she, wife of Elkanah's heart, could also give him children! Yet year after year when the family went up to the house of the Lord, Peninnah provoked Hannah until she wept and did not eat.

Elkanah said, "Hannah, why do you weep? And why do you not eat? And why is your heart grieved? Am I not better to you than ten sons?"

She took comfort but sought out Eli, the priest, who sat by a post of the temple of the Lord. In bitterness of soul, she prayed and wept. She vowed that if the Lord of hosts would give her a male child, she would give him to the Lord all the days of his life, and no razor would touch his head.

Hannah spoke in her heart; her lips only moved. Eli thought she was drunk. Hannah quickly denied it. "No, my lord. . .I have drunk neither wine nor strong drink, but have poured out my soul before the Lord."

Eli told her to go in peace. The God of Israel would grant her petition. Hannah went her way. She ate, and sadness left her countenance.

Hannah conceived and bore a son. She called his name Samuel, saying, "Because I have asked him of the Lord." She did not go up to offer the yearly sacrifice and told Elkanah that when Samuel was weaned she would bring him before the Lord, where the child would abide forever. At that time, Hannah took the child to Eli, the priest, repeating her vow and dedicating Samuel to God. She praised God, saying none was as holy as the Lord and telling how her heart rejoiced.

Eli blessed Elkanah and Hannah, and the Lord visited her. She bore three sons and two daughters. The child Samuel grew before the Lord, bringing greater rejoicing than ever to his mother's heart as he ministered unto the Lord before Eli the priest.

When Samuel was still a lad, the Lord called him three times. Samuel did not yet know the Lord, neither was the word of the Lord yet revealed to him. He ran to Eli, who told him after the second time that if the voice came again, he should say, "Speak, Lord, for your servant is listening." Samuel did as instructed and the Lord told him many things, including that Eli would be judged for the iniquity of his sons. Samuel hesitated to tell his friend, but Eli insisted.

Eli only replied, "It is the Lord: Let Him do what seems good."

Samuel grew, and the Lord was with him. All Israel from Dan even to Beersheba knew Samuel was established to be a prophet of the Lord.

As gracious as the meaning of her name, Hannah continued to be faithful. Surely in her secret mother heart she missed and yearned for the son God had given her, the son she returned to a life of service in fulfillment of her vow. Hannah wisely overcame her longings with praise and a continual song before the Lord, telling of His power and goodnepss. Her song was handed down throughout the ages and remains a shining testimony of pure mother love transcended only by love of the Lord God of Israel, almighty and everlasting.

1 Samuel 1–3

samuel, promised to God

Eli the high priest was almost blind when he was given a little boy named Samuel to raise in Shiloh. Samuel served him well, but Eli's own sons—priests like their father—were selfish and disrespectful of God. God determined to punish the family.

One night while Samuel was sleeping, the Lord called him

by name. Samuel thought the voice he heard must be Eli's, so he rose and went to Eli's bedside. "What do you need?" he asked the priest.

"I didn't call you," Eli said grumpily. "Go back to sleep."

After Samuel had settled into his bedding, the Lord called his name again. Again he went to Eli and asked, "What do you want?" And again the agitated priest sent Samuel back to bed.

When it happened a third time and Samuel appeared at his bedside, Eli realized God was calling Samuel. "Go back to bed," Eli told him. "If you hear the voice, say 'I hear you, Lord. What do you want?'"

Samuel did as he was told, and the Lord gave him a dreadful message. God said that Eli and his family were going to be punished forever because of the disrespect of Eli's sons. Understandably, Samuel did not want to share this news with his mentor. But Eli demanded to know what God had said to him. So Samuel relayed the prophecy to him.

"He is God," Eli acknowledged sadly. "He will do the right thing."

As Samuel grew to manhood, God appeared to him with more messages. The people realized Samuel was God's prophet. In fact, Samuel became the last great judge of the Israelites.

Samuel made judges of his own sons. But like the sons of Eli, they were ungodly. The Israelites did not want to follow them, and they demanded that Samuel in his old age appoint a king to rule the nation. This was not what the Lord wanted. Samuel warned them, but they insisted. So Samuel anointed a king for them. His name was Saul.

For a time, Saul was a good leader who protected his people. But eventually he turned away from God. Then God told Samuel, "I'm sorry I made Saul king of My people." He sent Samuel to the house of Jesse to find another king. Jesse's youngest son, David, would become Israel's greatest leader, but he was just a boy when Samuel privately anointed him to succeed the reigning King Saul.

---

1 Samuel; 2 Samuel

The young man Saul, son of Kish, was a head taller than any other Israelite. This handsome young man was introduced to Samuel, the prophet/judge who would bring him to power. Saul and his servant were looking for some escaped donkeys and were on the verge of giving up. The servant suggested they find the prophet Samuel and see if he could point them to their donkeys.

Samuel did much more than that. With a jar of olive oil, he anointed Saul king of the land! The Holy Spirit took hold of Saul, and he danced and shouted.

At first, Saul diligently sought the Lord's guidance and victoriously led the Israelites into battle against their enemies. But on one critical occasion, he failed to follow God's instructions carefully and it cost him his kingship.

Samuel told Saul that God wanted to punish the Amalekites for their past opposition to the Hebrews. "Attack them and destroy them," Samuel ordered the king. "Leave none of them, young or old, alive. Kill even the babies. Kill all their domestic animals, too."

Saul's soldiers attacked and slaughtered the Amalekites and took their king prisoner. But Saul failed to carry out God's command. He let the heathen king live. Moreover, his men killed only the weakest sheep and cattle and held back the choicest livestock, ostensibly to offer as sacrifices to the Lord.

God was very displeased with Saul. He had given Saul victory over Israel's longtime enemy, and Saul had responded with disobedience. God sent Samuel to inform the king that God hereby rejected him. God then sent the prophet to secretly anoint David as the future successor.

Saul brought the youthful David into his service as a court musician. David soon won the heart of the nation in his famous encounter with the Philistine giant Goliath. Saul became paranoid and jealous of David. He sensed that the young man might take his place and wanted to kill him. Soon, David and his growing legions of followers were driven into exile by King Saul.

Interestingly, it wasn't David or any of his men who ultimately ended Saul's life. In fact, David—on more than one occasion—let Saul live when he easily could have killed his tormentor. Rather, Saul and his sons died in a battle against Israel's fierce rivals, the Philistines. Although it brought his persecution to an end, Saul's death did not make David happy. Rather, he wrote a heartrending lament for Saul.

1 Samuel 9–31

jonathan, friend of david

How hard it must be to have a friend who is also your father's enemy—especially if your father is the most powerful man in the country. This was Jonathan's predicament. When the young shepherd David killed Goliath, Saul, king of Israel, brought David into his service. At that time Jonathan, Saul's son, gave David his clothing and armor as tokens, and they became loyal friends.

Jonathan's allegiance soon saved David's life. Saul knew the Lord loved David, and he was afraid God would replace him with the youngster. David won many battles over the Philistines, Israel's great foe, and his popularity disturbed Saul and stirred his jealousy. He became obsessed with the thought of killing David. Jonathan tried to change Saul's mind by gently reminding him of David's valuable service. Saul agreed not to hurt David—but this promise was soon forgotten.

Saul's anger toward David became uncontrollable, so Jonathan stepped in to help David escape. Jonathan knew David was going to become king, and he wanted to serve as David's right-hand man. They swore before God to always be loyal and helpful to each other and to each other's family.

Sadly, this was not to be. In a battle against the Philistines at Mount Gilboa, Saul was killed along with Jonathan and two of Saul's other sons. David grieved long for Jonathan and even for the relentless Saul. David wrote "The Song of the Bow" about Saul and Jonathan and required that everyone in Judah learn it. To David, Jonathan was his brother, and he lamented the loss of such a faithful friend.

_____

1 Samuel 13:3–4; 13:16–14:46; 18:1–4; 19:1–7, 20; 23:16-18; 31:1–5; 2 Samuel 1:1–27

david and his sheep

"Come here, little lamb!" David, the shepherd boy, called while hurrying after a lamb that had strayed from the flock he was keeping in his father Jesse's fields near Bethlehem. "Don't you know better than to leave your mother and go off by yourself?"

The naughty lamb, who wanted to run and play, didn't stop even long enough to look back at her keeper. "Baaaaa," she said and ran faster than ever.

David groaned. He had been taught since childhood that when lambs and sheep separated themselves from the flock, they were in great danger. Wild animals lurked outside herds of sheep. If a bear or lion saw the little lamb all alone, she could well become his dinner.

"Come back, I say!" David ordered. The lamb didn't stop. David looked at the other sheep. All except the lamb were peacefully eating grass. David sighed. He hated leaving them, but he had no choice. Father Jesse had sent him to tend sheep because he trusted his son to care for them. Now, even though it meant leaving the body of the flock unprotected, he must go find and restore the wayward lamb to the fold. With an anxious glance at the large herd of animals, he set off to capture the frolicking lamb.

Before he got far, a plaintive "Baaaaa, baaaaa!" sent David racing in the direction from which the cries were coming. His heart pounded. This "baaaaa" was *not* the sound of a lamb leaping for joy. It was the sound of a lamb in danger, frantically crying out for help, a cry David had heard many times.

David soon discovered why the terrified lamb was bleating. A lion had grabbed her in his mouth and was carrying her off!

"Stop!" David shouted at the top of his voice.

The lion looked back at the boy but didn't release the lamb. He just continued on his way, still holding the bleating lamb in his mouth.

David lifted the rod he always carried to protect his flock from danger. "Please, God, help me save the lamb," he prayed. Strengthened by his prayer and by days and nights of herding his flock in all kinds of weather, David brought his rod down with all his might. It struck the lion a terrible blow.

The lion opened his mouth to roar his rage. David grabbed the lamb out of his jaws. The lion turned on David, but the shepherd boy grabbed the lion's long hair. He hit him with the rod again and again, until the lion fell down dead.

David took the lamb in his arms. She was so scared that she shook all over. David carried her back to the flock and set her by her mother. "Baaaaa," she cried. David laughed. That frightened little lamb wouldn't be leaving her mother and running away again for a long, long time.

Lions weren't the only thing David, keeper of the flocks, had to fear on behalf of his charges. Now and then a bear would come looking for an easy meal. Lambs were the best targets because of their small size and inability to defend themselves. David was able to rescue a lamb from a bear in the same way he had saved the lamb caught in the lion's mouth. He prayed to God for help, then took up his rod and struck the bear with it until the lamb was saved.

---

1 Samuel 16–17

Samuel, the boy who heard God's voice and became a prophet, lived to be a very old man. His sons became judges over Israel, but they did not walk in the ways of the Lord. They took bribes and perverted judgment.

The people rose up in protest. They demanded that Samuel give them a king to rule over them, as other nations had.

Samuel was displeased. When he prayed, the Lord told Samuel, "The people have not rejected you but Me, that I should not reign over them. Tell them what manner of king will rule them."

Samuel did as directed. He warned the people of the consequences of their demands, but they refused to obey his warning, saying, "We will have a king over us who will judge us and go out before us and fight our battles."

God told Samuel to give them what they desired. He chose Saul, of whom it was said there was not a goodlier person among the children of Israel. Saul was powerful and a head taller than any of the people. Samuel anointed Saul and set him apart as king. Saul became a mighty leader, but after a time, he sinned and broke the commandments because he feared the people and obeyed them rather than God. Samuel rebuked Saul and warned him that the Lord had rejected him from being king.

One day God said to Samuel, "Go to Bethlehem. There you will find the king I have chosen among the sons of Jesse."

Even though Samuel knew that Saul would kill him if he discovered where he was going and why, Samuel obeyed. He reached Bethlehem and went to the home of Jesse. "Bring me your sons," he commanded.

First to come was Eliab. Surely this was the man the Lord had chosen to one day replace Saul. But God said, "Look not on the countenance or the height of his stature. The Lord does not see as man sees. Man looks on the outward appearance, but the Lord looks on the heart."

One by one, seven of Jesse's sons stepped forward. God did not choose any of them to be the new king.

"Have you more sons?" Samuel asked.

"Only David, my youngest. He is in the fields caring for the sheep," Jesse said.

"Send for him," Samuel ordered.

David didn't know what to think when his father sent word for him to leave the sheep and come to the house. He didn't think he had done anything wrong. Why, then, would Father Jesse send for him?

When David came to Samuel, God told the old prophet that David was the one. Samuel put oil on David's head and said a prayer. David would be king of Israel when he grew up.

God's Spirit came into the boy's heart. He had never felt so happy or excited.

David could play the harp, as well as take care of the sheep. One day the servants of King Saul came for David. "Our master has times of great trouble. Come play the harp for him so he can find peace."

Saul liked David so much that he kept him at the palace part of the time. Whenever Saul felt sick, David played his harp. It always made Saul feel better.

When David came to the king's palace, he met Jonathan, Saul's son. They immediately became such strong friends that when Jonathan learned his father had grown jealous of David and planned to kill him, he warned his friend and saved his life.

1 Samuel 16

david meets a giant

King Saul was at his wit's end. He paced the floor of his palace, shaking his head and roaring demands for his counselors to advise him. The Philistines, longtime enemies of God's people, were preparing to attack Saul's armies. They stood on a mountain on one side of a valley, while the Israelites stood on a mountain across from them. Even worse, the biggest and meanest of their rank taunted Saul's army every day for forty days, calling for someone to come fight him.

"Send me a man, any man," he bellowed. "If he is able to fight me and win, we will be your servants. If I slay him, you will serve us. I defy the armies of Israel this day. Give me a man to fight."

"You have many brave men in your army," Saul's counselors reminded him. "Three of them are the brothers of David, the shepherd boy. Your men are loyal, as well. Yet tell us, mighty King, how can any man fight Goliath? He is over nine feet tall, and he has brothers almost as tall as he!"

King Saul was sorely grieved, but he had no answer.

One day Jesse told his youngest son, "Take this grain and these loaves of bread to your brothers in the camp of Saul. Give these cheeses to their leaders and bring me word of my sons."

David rose early in the morning, left his sheep with a keeper, and headed for the battlefield. He reached the Israelite army just as they were preparing themselves to fight against the Philistines. David left his food with the man in charge of provisions and ran into the battle lines to find his brothers.

Suddenly Goliath rose to his full height, towering above lesser men. He wore full armor that covered him from head to toe, except for his sneering face. "Send someone to fight me," he bawled. His loud, frightening voice scared King Saul's men. They turned and ran away!

David did not run away. "I will fight the giant," he said.

King Saul could scarcely believe his ears. "What do you say?" He shook his head in disbelief. "You, a mere boy? What foolishness is this?"

David refused to be intimidated by the king. "I have killed a lion and a bear that attacked my sheep," he said. "The God who saved me from the wild animals will save me now."

David's older brother Eliab was furious. "What are you doing here, anyway? Who is taking care of the sheep in the wilderness? I know how proud you are and how rebellious. You have come to see the battle."

The argument raged until at last King Saul agreed to let David fight. He armed the boy with his own armor, but David laid it aside.

When Goliath saw David, the giant was enraged. He, fight a boy?

David cried, "I fight you in the name of the Lord. All the world will know there is a God in Israel. The battle is the Lord's. This day He will give you all into our hands." David took a stone from his bag. He put it in his slingshot and let it fly. *Wham!* It hit the wicked giant and killed him.

Goliath crashed to the ground so hard that it shook. His unexpected defeat frightened the enemies, and they ran away. God had helped the shepherd boy who would one day be king of all Israel to save His people—just as He had helped David save the little lambs from the lion and the bear.

1 Samuel 17

michal, daughter of saul

Michal, younger daughter of King Saul, loved David from the first time she saw him. Yet she knew she must lay her love aside. Her father had promised David the hand of Merab, his elder daughter. All of Michal's inner rebellion could not change things. She considered going to her father but hastily put aside the thought. Everyone knew of the rages that came upon Saul. Michal shuddered. She dared not chance having his wrath turned toward her.

Much had happened since the day David, son of Jesse, first

stood before Saul. Ruddy, attractive to look on, his beautiful countenance attracted both Saul and young Michal. The king sent to Jesse, saying, "Let David stand before me, for he has found favor in my sight."

From that time on when the evil spirit entered Saul, David played softly on his harp. The music soothed the king and refreshed him, and he became well. Saul loved David greatly and made him his armor bearer.

Michal sighed. When did the corrosion of envy begin to enter Saul's heart, leaving it open to the evil spirit that vexed him? She sadly shook her head. Perhaps when the young shepherd went forth against the mighty Philistine, Goliath. A tender look of remembrance crossed Michal's face, and a smile curved her lips. David had thrown aside the king's own armor, a helmet of brass and a coat of mail. Taking five smooth stones and his sling, he slew the giant.

How her father had praised him—then. Michal thrilled at David's bravery. She thought of how her own brother Jonathan's very soul was knit with the soul of David. Her dark eyes glowed. Jonathan had stripped himself of garments, sword, and bow and given them to David as a token of the covenant of brotherhood between them.

Sadness replaced Michal's smile. Saul set David over his soldiers, and all Israel and Judah loved David. A pang of fear went through her. She had seen her father's anger when the new young leader returned from the slaughter of the Philistines. Women came out of all the cities of Israel, singing and dancing, saying as they played on instruments, "Saul has slain his thousands, and David his ten thousands."

The next day while in the throes of an evil spirit, Saul threw a javelin and barely missed killing the young man he had loved until mistrust changed everything. He grew afraid of David because the Lord was with him and had departed from Saul. The king made him captain over a thousand and sent him from his presence. At that time, Saul also promised Merab to David.

Michal felt hot shame when her father broke his vow and

gave Merab to another, but she could not deny the spirit of joy that rose within her when Saul decided to give her to David instead. Nothing could make her happier.

Saul, the man God had called to reign over His people, had changed into a treacherous, bitter king. Jonathan stood between father and friend, true to his vow. Michal saved her husband's life when Saul's men came after him by letting him down through a window. She put the form of a man in her bed and said David lay sick when Saul sent messengers to take him.

Did Michal's heart break when her father gave her as wife to Phalti after David became an outlaw? And when David took first Abigail and then Ahinoam as his wives? After Saul's death and David's anointing as king of Judah, he demanded Michal be returned to him. The Bible says her weeping husband went with her until he was sent back.

What memories filled the heart that had once been wholly David's? It appears love fled sometime over the years. Michal railed against David when she saw him leaping and dancing in front of the people. He responded by reminding her he was the king, chosen by the Lord. He vowed to be even viler. No wonder God had to give David a new heart before the shepherd who became king could change into the man God needed.

Michal had no children by David.

---

1 Samuel 18–19; 2 Samuel 3, 6

abigail, wife of nabal

Few men were more blessed than Nabal. He owned three thousand sheep and a thousand goats. In addition, his wife, Abigail, not only had a beautiful countenance, but possessed good understanding. Nabal should have sung praises for all that was his as he sheared his sheep in Carmel. The churlish man did not and was known for his evil doings.

David, in the wilderness, mourning for Samuel's death, heard of Nabal. He called out ten young men and said, "Go up to Carmel, and go to Nabal, and greet him in my name." He went on to tell them to extend peace to Nabal and his house and all he had and to remind Nabal how well David had treated the shepherds while they were in Carmel.

David finished his instructions by telling the young men to say, "Give, I pray you, whatever comes to your hand to your servants, and to your son David."

Nabal listened to the words of David as given by the young men, then sneered. "Who is David? And who is the son of Jesse? Many servants nowadays are breaking away from their masters. Shall I then take my bread, and my water, and my meat that I have killed for my shearers, and give it to men, coming from who knows where?"

This angered David greatly. He ordered four hundred of his men to gird themselves with their swords and follow him.

One of the young men who served Nabal witnessed the exchange. He told Abigail that David had sent messengers out of the wilderness to salute the master but that Nabal railed against them. He went on to tell her of David and his men's kindness and protection to Nabal's shepherds when they were in the field. Nothing of Nabal's was missing during all the time they tended the sheep. "They were a wall to us both by night and day, all the while we were with them keeping the sheep," he earnestly reported. "Know and consider what you will do; for evil is determined against our master and against all of his household, for he is such a son of Belial* that a man cannot speak to him."

Anger at her husband's treatment of David's messengers surged through Abigail. She immediately took great quantities of food and loaded them on donkeys. She said nothing of her plan to Nabal but followed her servants. Heart beating in time with the hooves of the donkey she rode, she came down the hill and met David and his followers. Abigail dismounted and fell at his feet to beg for mercy. She told him she had been given no knowledge of the rude way his men were treated and offered the food she had brought. She prophesied of the great things the Lord God of Israel would one day do with David.

David rejoiced that Abigail had kept him from shedding blood. He sent her to her house in peace. She found Nabal holding a great feast and drunken with wine. She told him nothing until the next day. His heart failed when he heard those things, and ten days later he died.

Abigail later became David's wife. The mists of time obscure most of her life after that. We know she was one of many wives, bore a son called Chileab, was taken captive by the Amalekites, and then was rescued by David. Did she maintain the high courage that first brought her to David's attention? The beautiful countenance? Or did years of having to share her husband with other women slowly grind her down? The story of how she lived up to the meaning of her name, "of strength," serves as an example of one unafraid to face the enemy and conquer by reasoning, rather than the use of weapons.

*Belial: wicked, worthless

---

1 Samuel 25, 27, 30

joab, military leader

Civil war was brewing. King Saul was dead and the people of Judah wanted David to be their king. Meanwhile, to the north in Israel, the army commander Abner had made Saul's son Ishbosheth a puppet king; Abner himself held the real power. Men who once respected each other had become enemies.

Joab and his brothers Abishai and Asahel were warriors for David. But Abner killed Joab's brother Asahel, and Joab was angered when Abner made a pact with David. Without David's knowledge, Joab arranged a meeting with Abner and murdered him in cold blood. Dismayed, David ordered his people to mourn for Abner and prayed that God would punish Joab and his family.

This set the tone of David and Joab's relationship. When David became king of all Israel, Joab was the commander of his army. Joab proved to be a clever, brave military leader who always wanted to do what he thought was best for David. But he sometimes did things his own way and was never afraid to speak his mind to the king. For example, David's rebellious son Absalom tried to take over the kingship. A battle ensued, and David wanted his soldiers to let Absalom live. But Joab knew David's softheartedness would only result in future trouble with Absalom. So, while Absalom hung by his hair, helpless in a tree, Joab killed him.

At the end of David's reign, Joab allied himself with David's son Adonijah, who wanted to take over the throne. David instead chose his son Solomon to succeed him. On his deathbed David cited Joab's disrespect to Solomon. "Punish him as you will," David said. "Do not let him die in peace."

Solomon wasted little time securing his position as king. He dispatched Benaiah, who had been the captain of David's guard and would become Solomon's army commander, to kill Adonijah and Joab. And so, this clever player in the game of politics and war ultimately was paid in violence for his choices.

---

2 Samuel 2:8–3:39; 8:15–18; 10:1–14; 11:1–25; 12:26–27; 14:1–33; 18:1–19:7; 20:6–23; 1 Kings 1:1–2:35; 1 Chronicles 11:6–8; 19:8–15; 20:1; 21:1–7

nathan, bold prophet

"Why have you trampled on the Lord's laws and done this evil?" said the prophet to the king. This booming indictment came in response to a serious deed that called into question the sinner's regard for God Almighty. Few people would have the nerve to talk to a king this way. But Nathan the prophet knew that the sin of King David was so great the hills would have roared in anguish had it gone unreproved.

David fell in love with Bathsheba, the wife of a Hittite warrior named Uriah who fought in David's army. Not only so, but David had committed adultery with Bathsheba. To lawfully remove Bathsheba's husband so he could marry her, David ordered Joab, the commander of his army, to place Uriah in the thick of battle. Then, to make doubly sure Uriah died, David had his general arrange for the army to withdraw suddenly and leave Uriah alone against the enemy. This was nothing short of murder. After Uriah's death, David took the widow Bathsheba for his wife.

The prophet Nathan became aware of the king's sinfulness and soon arrived in the palace to tell David this story: A rich man owned many cows and sheep. In the same town a poor man lived who owned just one little lamb. The lamb meant a lot to the poor man and his family. In fact, it was their pet. One day the rich man began to prepare a banquet, but he did not want to kill any of his own animals for the meal. So he stole the poor man's lamb, cooked it, and served it to his guests.

David was furious at the fictitious rich man. Then Nathan interpreted, "You are that rich man."

Nathan told David that because of his bloody treachery with Uriah and Bathsheba, David's own family would reap a bloody reward. "This will never again be a peaceful house," Nathan promised.

David repented, and the Lord did not punish him by death. But the newborn son, conceived in David and Bathsheba's adultery, did not live.

---

2 Samuel 7:1–17; 12:1–15, 24–25; 1 Kings 1:10–45; 1 Chronicles 17:1–15; 29:29; 2 Chronicles 9:29; 29:25

"What shall I do?" The distraught woman hugged her arms across her breast and rocked to and fro. Fear smote her, tasting metallic in her mouth. "I shall be stoned, even though the king himself be responsible for my plight." The thought settled her whirling brain. Hope crept into her troubled face. Surely David would not allow such a thing to happen! Making haste, she sent a message by a trusted servant, four short words.

King David curiously opened the missive and read, "I am with child." He laid it aside, remembering. After the year of peace that had been declared, he sent Joab, his servants, and all Israel forth to battle, but David tarried at Jerusalem. One evening, he arose from his bed to walk on the roof of his house. He looked down from his lofty domain and his blood ran hot, for a lovely woman washed herself. He must discover who she was.

"Bathsheba, wife of Uriah the Hittite," came the reply.

Her married status could not quell the fire of David's desire. He commanded that she be brought to him. Now she had conceived. What could he do? Even a king was not exempt from the punishment for adultery, which was death.

A scheme formed in his mind. He would bring Uriah back from fighting and send him to his wife so that the evil David had done might not be discovered.

David's plan did not work. Uriah came but slept at the door of the king's house with the servants. A conscientious soldier, he would not go to his home and wife while the ark of the covenant and his master Joab and fellow companions camped in the open fields.

David hastily sent him back to Joab, carrying a letter that ordered the commander to put Uriah in the forefront of the hottest battle and leave him there to be smitten and die. Joab obeyed, and it came to pass.

Bathsheba mourned for the husband she had lost, guilt-ridden, secretly glad he never knew that which had come upon her. When her mourning time ended, David took her as his wife. But the thing David had done displeased the Lord.

Fear again filled Bathsheba when Nathan posed a riddle to the king that showed clearly he knew on whose order Uriah had died. Nathan made a terrible pronouncement: Evil would rise against David out of his own house, and all Israel would know.

The child Bathsheba had born unto David fell ill and on the seventh day died. Her mother heart filled with anguish. This, then, was the price to be paid for sin. Not until David comforted her and she bore another son called Solomon did Bathsheba's sad heart find joy again. Years later, when David was old, she fought for her son Solomon to be named king in place of Adonijah, who even then was taking over, for David was stricken in years and knew not what was happening. People were crying, "God save King Adonijah." King David swore by the Lord God of Israel that Solomon would sit on the throne in his stead. He ordered Solomon to be anointed as ruler over Israel and Judah.

Bathsheba bowed with her face to the earth. Triumph filled her soul. She honored the king and said, "Let my lord, King David, live forever."

After David's death, Solomon ascended to the throne. Adonijah sought her out, saying he came in peace. He asked her to intercede with King Solomon that he might be given Abishag, David's Shunammite concubine, as his wife.

Bathsheba agreed. Solomon seated her at his right hand but grew enraged when she made the request. He told her she might as well have asked the kingdom and ordered that Adonijah be executed unless he bowed down to the rightful king, which he did. Nothing more is known of Bathsheba.

2 Samuel 11–12; 1 Kings 2

David reigned over Israel for forty years: seven in Hebron and thirty-three in Jerusalem. He experienced defeat and victory, sorrow and joy. When he turned away from God and followed his own sinful desires, troubles poured down on him, but when he fell on his knees and repented, God forgave him.

God also blessed David with a special son named Solomon, which means "peaceable." When King David grew old, he proclaimed that Solomon would be king over all Israel. He blessed Solomon and laid on him the responsibility of ruling the people. "Be strong, my son," he charged. "Show yourself a man. Do all the Lord requires. Walk in His ways. Keep His statutes and commandments, His judgments and testimonies, which are written in the Law of Moses. If you do this, you will prosper in everything you do. Your kingdom will be far greater than my own."

Soon after, David died, and Solomon ascended to the throne. He loved the Lord and showed his love by living in accordance with his father's teachings.

One night in Gibeon, the Lord came to Solomon in a dream. "Ask what I shall give you."

Solomon replied, "You have shown my father, David, mercy as he walked before You in truth and righteousness. You gave him a son to sit on the throne. Lord, You have made me king instead of David." He sighed. "I am but a little child. I don't even know how to go out or come in. I am among the people You have chosen, so many they cannot be counted." He paused, then said, "I ask You to give me an understanding heart, so that I may judge wisely and separate good from bad—for who can judge such a great many of Your people?"

God was pleased that Solomon had humbly confessed his inadequacy and asked for help instead of seeking something for himself. He said, "Because you asked for understanding and have not sought long life, great riches, or the death of your enemies,

I will do according to your wishes. I have given you a wise and understanding heart. None who came before you, or shall rise after you, shall be like you. I will also give you what you did *not* seek: riches and honor. If you will follow Me, as your father David did, I will lengthen your days."

Solomon awakened, knowing that God would surely give him the wisdom to judge.

His wisdom was tested a short time later. Two women came before him, both claiming to be the mother of the same child. They had delivered their babies just three days apart, in the same house. That night one of the babies died. One woman cried, "When this woman discovered that her child was dead, she laid him in my arms and stole my living baby!"

The other screamed, "It is not so! The child is mine."

Back and forth they argued, while Solomon pondered what to do. At last he said, "Bring a sword. Divide the baby into two parts and give one to each of the women."

A river of tears flowed down the real mother's face. "Don't kill my baby, my lord!" she pleaded. "Give it to her."

"Let it be neither hers nor mine," the other woman said. "Divide it."

"Do not kill the baby," Solomon thundered. "Give it to the first woman. She is his mother."

All Israel heard of Solomon's judgment and feared the king. They saw that the wisdom of God was within him to bring justice.

---

1 Kings 3

the queen of sheba meets solomon

Solomon's fame spread to the uttermost ends of the known earth. Tales of his wealth and wisdom ran far and wide. People spoke of his wisdom, which came about in this manner:

In Gibeon the Lord appeared to Solomon in a dream and said, "Ask what I shall give thee."

Solomon rehearsed the great mercy God had shown to his father, David, according to when he walked in truth, righteousness, and uprightness of heart. God had kept for David great kindness, even a son to sit on his throne.

"I am but a little child," Solomon confessed. "I know not how to go out or come in. Your servant is in the midst of Your people whom You have chosen, a great people, that cannot be numbered nor counted for multitude. Give therefore Your servant an understanding heart to judge Your people, that I may discern between good and bad. For who is able to judge so great a people?"

The request pleased God. He promised that since Solomon had not asked for wealth or long life or the life of his enemies, there would be none like Solomon either before or after. God also blessed Solomon abundantly with the riches he had not sought, with honor and length of days.

In faraway Arabia, the Queen of Sheba rested on soft cushions and narrowed her painted eyelids. Who was this Solomon, this man whose praise was sung by every passing caravan? She surveyed her surroundings. Did he, then, possess more than she? Was his palace more splendid, his robes of grander fabric and design? She laughed, mocking the thought. Did not the world know none was so mighty as the Queen of Sheba?

Yet a note of jealousy marred the laugh and with it a daring idea. Why should she not go to Jerusalem and see for herself? A single clap of the hands would bring a bevy of servants ready to do her bidding. Stay. She must consider well before embarking on the journey.

The queen's curiosity waxed hotter with every wild tale. Even allowing for certain exaggeration, the kingdom of Solomon loomed ever more appealing in her mind. At last she ordered a great train to be prepared, camels bearing spices, quantities of gold, and precious stones. When she reached Jerusalem, she decked herself out in her finest apparel and came to Solomon.

Armed with questions, the queen shot them at the ruler whose fame had spread like fire in a field of ripe and waving wheat. Her all-seeing eyes saw the splendor of his house, the food, all who served him, even the way by which he went up unto the house of the Lord. She hated to admit defeat, but what she saw forced her to do so. She said, "I believed not the words until I came. . . . Behold, the half was not told me: Your wisdom and prosperity exceed the fame which I heard. Happy are your men, your servants who stand continually before you and hear your wisdom. Blessed be the Lord your God, who delights in you, to set you on the throne of Israel. Because the Lord loved Israel forever, therefore He made you king, to do judgment and justice."

The Queen of Sheba gave Solomon great riches, but he gave her all her desire, whatever she asked, besides that which Solomon gave her of his royal bounty. She and her servants turned and went to her own country.

Scripture records that the magnificence of Solomon's court impressed the queen until "there was no more spirit in her." Perhaps this best shows the extent to which God blessed the king with material possessions. The magnitude of Solomon's wisdom, power, and honor cannot be measured.

---

1 Kings 10

jezebel, idolatrous queen

Ahab, son of Omri, reigned over Israel twenty-two years. It is written he "did evil in the eyes of the Lord and sinned more than all those before him," surpassing the wickedness of anyone up to that time. Marrying Jezebel and embracing her gods ranked first on his list of sins.

The name Jezebel has been known throughout history as a

synonym for dark deeds and treachery. It is not hard to picture a scene such as this:

Jezebel, silken, perfumed, jeweled, lolling on richly embroidered cushions. Painted face. Long fingernails stained as red as if dipped in blood. Physically beautiful enough to tempt any man not dedicated to a God higher than those she served. A hundred plots milling in her scheming, clever brain. A dozen maidens clustered around her, freakish imitations of Jezebel's sensuous charm.

"I will marry Ahab himself," she predicts. Her eyes glitter with assurance of her power over men. "I shall be queen of all Israel. What better way to establish the true religion, the worship of Baal?"

A murmur ripples through the bevy of maidens, but no one dares disagree. Jezebel's streak of cruelty and supreme vanity permit no criticism. She reigns over her private kingdom by fear, not by the admiration of those who serve and fawn upon her.

"Ahab shall build a house of Baal in Samaria and set up an altar to him." Jezebel whips herself into a frenzy. Hot color pours into her cheeks, and a gleam that spells disaster for anyone who gets in her way comes to her eyes. "Ahab shall also make a grove. . . ." She allows her voice to trail off, and a self-satisfied smirk tilts her red, red lips.

The maidens clap their hands. Their eyes glisten. Only too well do they know the dancing, cavorting, and unholy actions in the groves dedicated to the heathen gods the Israelites despise. "Will such a thing not provoke the God of Ahab?" one, more daring than the rest, asks.

Affronted, Jezebel sternly reminds them, "There is no god like Baal." She sinks her white teeth into her painted lower lip and plans more evil.

How she rejoices when Ahab does as she asks! How she boasts. She cuts off the prophets of the Lord, all except the hundred Obadiah spirits away, hides in a cave, and feeds bread and water. She laughs at famine and drought, little caring that many suffer because of her and Ahab. She hates Elijah with all the fury of one who knows her own vileness but will not tolerate anyone speaking of it. If fear crosses her mind when he challenges her gods, she hides it and exultantly anticipates the confrontation on Mount Carmel between her 450 prophets of Baal and 400 of the grove. This day Baal will defeat the Israelite God forever!

It does not happen. All morning, the prophets cry for Baal to send fire and consume the offering on the altar. Nothing happens, even though they scream until hoarse and leap on the altar.

At noon Elijah mocks the false prophets, taunting that their gods must be asleep or talking or perhaps away on a journey. The priests slash their bodies, and Jezebel shrieks at them to conquer. That evening Elijah builds an altar in the name of the Lord. Three times it is soaked with water. After a simple prayer, fire comes from heaven and consumes everything, including the water in the trench. The people fall on their faces, crying, "The Lord, He is the God." Elijah slays every false prophet, and the rain returns.

Jezebel's fury knows no bounds when Ahab tells her what has happened. She threatens Elijah's life and laughs when he prophesies her violent end. Years later, vain to the last, she paints her face and taunts Jehu, the new king, from her window. Perhaps she feels her aging charms will save her. Is there regret in her heart when the eunuchs who sympathize with Jehu lift her up and throw her from the window? If so, is it for her wickedness or only her loss of power and life? No one knows. . .and as Elijah prophesied, the dogs wait below.

1 Kings 16, 18–19; 2 Kings 9

the zerephath widow and elijah—miraculous meals

Only a poor widow, her name is unknown to those who handed down her story from generation to generation. Yet the widow who dwelled in Zerephath is revered by all who meet her in the first book of Kings. She gave all. Not because she could afford to give. The widow could not afford not to give.

God sent ravens to feed Elijah during the famine by which he was punishing Israel, telling him to hide by the brook Cherith and drink from it. The brook dried up for lack of rain in the land, so God sent Elijah to Zerephath, saying, "I have commanded a widow woman there to sustain thee."

When Elijah reached the gate of the city, a widow woman bent low, gathering sticks. He called to her. "Fetch me, I pray thee, a little water in a vessel, that I may drink." She started to obey, and he called again, "Bring me, I pray thee, a morsel of bread in thine hand."

The widow stared at him. If only she could! Offering water was one thing; sharing food was another. Her thin hands trembled, and she thought of the final bit of food in her possession. "As the Lord thy God liveth, I have not a cake, but an handful of meal in a barrel, and a little oil in a cruse. . . . I am gathering two sticks that I may go in and dress it for me and my son, that we may eat it, and die."

"Fear not," Elijah told her. "Go and do as thou hast said. But make and bring me a little cake first, and after make for thee and for thy son. For thus saith the Lord God of Israel, 'The barrel of meal shall not waste, neither shall the cruse of oil fail, until the day that the Lord sendeth rain upon the earth.'"

The widow could scarcely believe her ears. Who was this stranger to promise such a thing? Was it a deception to gain the last of her food? She looked into his face. Something caused her to do his bidding. She slowly took out the meal and oil to make a cake for the stranger, but there yet remained other meal and oil. She marveled, prepared food for herself and her child, and thanked the God of Israel. For many days, each time the household hungered, the widow closed her eyes in fear, then rejoiced and baked cakes from the never-empty barrel and cruse.

Her blessings did not end with food. After these things, the widow's son fell ill until his breath left him. She called out in pain, asking why Elijah had done so unto her. He took the child to a loft and laid him upon the bed. He then cried to the Lord, stretched himself upon the child three times, and said, "O Lord my God, I pray thee, let this child's soul come into him again."

Elijah took the child and brought him down out of the chamber into the house and delivered him unto his mother. He said, "See, thy son liveth."

The widow raised her head, bowed with weeping. She stilled her mourning and received her child with great joy. Her heart overflowed with gratefulness, and she said unto Elijah, "Now by this I know that thou art a man of God, and that the word of the Lord in thy mouth is truth."

And it all began with a handful of meal and a little oil in a cruse.

---

1 Kings 17

elisha helps the children

God called many prophets to warn the people that they must repent. In his old age, Elijah was told by God to set Elisha apart as a prophet. One day when they stood beside the river Jordan, with fifty sons of the prophets observing from a distance, Elijah rolled up his cloak and struck the water. The river parted, allowing the men to cross over on dry land.

Once on the other side, Elijah said, "I will soon be taken away from you. What shall I do for you before I go?"

Elisha replied, "Give me a double portion of your spirit, that it may be upon me."

Elijah said, "You have asked a hard thing, but if you see me when I am taken from you, it will be yours. If not, it will be denied."

While they walked and talked, God sent a chariot of fire and horses of fire. Elijah was carried up to heaven in a whirlwind!

Elisha saw what happened. He cried, "My father! My father! The chariot and horsemen of Israel!" He tore his clothes apart, knowing he would see Elijah no more. Then he picked up the cloak Elijah had dropped. He struck the water. Again it parted, and he safely crossed over.

The watching prophets knew that the spirit of Elijah was resting on Elisha.

Sometime afterward, a certain woman came to Elisha. "My husband, who was your servant, is dead," she cried. "You know he feared and honored the Lord. Now his creditor is demanding that my two sons become his slaves in order to pay my husband's debt."

"What do you have in your house?" Elisha questioned.

"Nothing except a pot of oil."

"Go to your neighbors," the prophet told her. "Borrow all the empty jars they will give you. Then go inside your house and shut the door. Pour oil from your vessel into the empty ones."

The woman stared at him and then did as she was told. Her sons watched in awe as the oil from her one pot filled every vessel. "We are out of jars," one son said.

"We are out of oil, too," the other added.

Elisha told them, "Go sell the oil. Pay your debt. There will be enough money left for you and your sons to live on."

---

2 Kings 2, 4

the shunammite woman hosts elisha

"Sir, I beg of you to eat bread with us," a woman of Shunem pleaded with Elisha when he came to her village.

Elisha turned aside and ate with the woman, who was highly

respected by all who knew her. She immediately beseeched the prophet to honor her home by eating with them whenever he came to Shunem. And so Elisha ate at the woman's table.

The good woman perceived he was a holy man of God, who passed by continually. She told her husband, "Let us make a little chamber, I pray thee, on the wall; and let us set for him there a bed, a table, a stool, and a candlestick: and it shall be, when he cometh to us, that he shall turn in thither."

The next time Elisha came, he entered the chamber and lay there. After a time he ordered his servant, Gehazi, "Call this Shunammite." When she stood before him, Elisha spoke of how carefully she had provided for him. He asked, "What is to be done for thee? Wouldst thou be spoken for to the king, or to the captain of the host?"

"I dwell among my own people," she answered.

Again Elisha asked, "What then is to be done for her?"

Gehazi, who had remained silent during the interchange, spoke. "Verily she hath no child, and her husband is old."

For the second time Elisha called her. When the woman stood in the door, he said, "About this season, according to the time of life, thou shalt embrace a son."

The woman stared at him, then shook her head. "Nay, my lord," she sadly replied. "Thou man of God, do not lie unto thine handmaid."

Great was her joy when even as Elisha had predicted, she conceived and bore a son in due season.

One day when the child grew older, he went out to his father, who was with the reapers. Suddenly he clutched his head and groaned.

"My head, my head!" Alarmed, his father ordered a lad to carry him to his mother. The stricken son sat on her knees till noon, then died. The good woman refused to accept his death. She laid him on Elisha's bed, shut the door, and went out. "Send me one of the young men," she ordered her grieving husband. "And one of the donkeys, that I may run to the man of God, and come again."

The husband couldn't understand. He asked why she would go on that day. But the great woman only said, "It shall be well." Commanding the young man driving the donkeys not to hesitate for her, she went and came unto Mount Carmel.

Gehazi, the servant, met her when she was yet afar off from the man of God. He told her Elisha had seen her and told him to inquire if all was well. She valiantly replied all was well but then caught Elisha by the feet when she came to him, in spite of Gehazi's protests. She refused to leave him until Elisha rose and followed her. Gehazi passed on before them and laid his master's staff on the child's face but came back wearing a long face. The child had not awakened. By the time Elisha came into the house, the child lay dead.

The Shunammite woman waited while Elisha went in, lay upon the child, with his mouth on the child's mouth, his eyes on his eyes, and his hands on his hands. The child's flesh grew warm. Elisha repeated the process. From outside the chamber, the woman heard a sneeze. Another, and another, seven in all. Her heart leaped within her breast. Surely her child lived! Elisha called her in. She beheld her son, then fell at the prophet's feet and bowed to the ground. The son granted by God's mercy had been spared.

---

2 Kings 4

the captive maid

"Why do you weep, my mistress?" a little captive maid of Israel, handmaiden in the house of Naaman, captain of the host of the king of Syria, timidly asked. Although she often longed for her own people, she had learned to love Naaman and his wife. He was an honorable man, respected by the king. By him the Lord had given deliverance unto Syria. He was also a mighty man in valor and kind to those who served him.

Now the little maid's mistress lay sobbing as if her heart would break. Again the girl asked, "Why do you weep?"

"Leprosy has come upon Naaman," his wife stammered.

Leprosy! Dreaded and feared by all. And yet the little maid's heart beat high. She spoke quickly. "Would God my lord were with the prophet who is in Samaria! For he would cure him of his leprosy."

The suffering woman raised dazed eyes to her maid, a feeble hope springing to her face. They scarcely noticed that one who overheard hastily left the chamber. The man repeated word for word what the little maid had said.

Naaman could scarcely believe it, yet anything was better than watching the awful sickness creep over him. He told the king of all Syria, who immediately sent him with a letter to the king of Israel, asking that he heal Naaman.

The Israelite king rent his clothes. He was not God; neither had he the power to cure leprosy.

Mistress and maid waited, hoped, and prayed. Day after day passed. Their hearts sang when Naaman returned to them. Not a trace of the terrible disease remained. The little maid stood near her mistress while he told his story.

"The king could do nothing, but a man named Elisha said for me to go to him. I came with my horses and chariot and stood by the door of his house." A rueful look crossed his face. "Elisha didn't even come outside. He sent a messenger telling me to go wash in the Jordan seven times, and my flesh would come again to me and I would be clean."

The little maid's eyes rounded. Her mistress gasped. "How strange! Did he not know who you were?" she disbelievingly asked.

"He had given his command," her husband told her. "I was angry, but I still thought he would come forth, call on the name of the Lord his God, and strike the leprosy from my body. If I must wash in a river, why the Jordan? Are not the rivers of Damascus better? When he did not come, I went away in a rage."

"But you are healed!" his wife protested.

Naaman's voice softened. Wonder came into his eyes. "Ah, my brave servants came near and said, 'My father, if the prophet had bidden you to do some great thing, would you not have done it? How much rather then, when he tells to you, wash and be clean?'

"I listened to them. I dipped myself in the Jordan. Once, twice, until I rose from the water six times. The leprosy remained." His face took on a look of awe. "The seventh time I rose straightway out of the water clean and purified! This time when I went to the prophet's house, he came out. I said to him that there is no God in all the earth but the God in Israel."

The little Israelite maid clapped her hands in joy. Many times she wondered, was it for this she had been taken into captivity? To be the instrument by which Naaman would find Elisha and be healed? The thought comforted her, and she continued to serve those who never tired of expressing appreciation that she had told them about the prophet of the true and living God.

2 Kings 5

hezekiah, faithful king

The Old Testament grimly testifies that Israel had its share of bad rulers. A refreshing exception was Hezekiah. His reign began around 710 BC when he was twenty-five years old. Hezekiah "did that which was right in the sight of the Lord." He was completely faithful. No other king before or after him was his peer in this regard. In return the Lord blessed him and helped him prevail against the enemies of Israel.

Hezekiah's greatest challenge came early in his reign when Assyria invaded Judah. "Don't listen to Hezekiah," the Assyrian commander told the frightened Israelites. "His God won't protect you. No other kingdoms have been able to withstand our might. Surrender to us, and live in peace." The Jews began to believe him and to doubt the wisdom and ability of their devout leader.

Hezekiah turned to the great prophet Isaiah for counsel, and Isaiah reassured him that the Lord had doomed the Assyrian invasion to confusion and failure. So it proved. King Sennacherib of Assyria returned to Ninevah and ultimately was murdered by his own sons.

King Hezekiah became deathly ill to the point that even Isaiah predicted he would die. But Hezekiah prayed; the Lord heard and sent Isaiah to announce that the king would live another fifteen years.

Though godly and faithful, Hezekiah did not always make wise decisions. While Hezekiah was sick, the king of Babylonia sent messengers bearing a gift. Gratified by this display of kindness, Hezekiah gave the Babylonian envoys a detailed tour of his country's storehouses and armaments. In fact, there was no strategic secret in all of Judah that Hezekiah didn't imprudently reveal to these seemingly friendly visitors. God told Hezekiah through Isaiah that the result of his carelessness would be the Babylonian conquest of Judah. This occurred a century later.

Hezekiah ruled for twenty-nine years. He was succeeded by his twelve-year-old son, Manasseh, who shunned his father's righteous ways and returned to the idol worship Hezekiah had denounced.

2 Kings 18–20

josiah, boy king

Many, many kings ruled over Israel. Some were good; others were not. Sometimes a new king would be set on the throne when he was quite young. Manasseh was only twelve when he began his fifty-five-year reign over Jerusalem. He followed the abominations of the heathen and built altars to strange gods, made graven images, and wrought much wickedness.

His son Amon was no better. Amon became king over Jerusalem when he was twenty-two and ruled for the next two years. He did not love or serve God. He followed the path of his father, Manasseh, and did all sorts of evil things. Worst of all, he turned from the Lord God of his ancestors and worshiped the idols his father worshiped, bowing down before them in defiance to the one true God.

The only good thing that came out of Amon's reign was his son Josiah. From the time Josiah was just a young boy, he loved and tried to please God, in spite of his father's terrible example. He did what was right in the sight of the Lord and walked in all the ways King David had proclaimed, not turning aside to either the right or the left.

This was not easy for Josiah. His heart ached because of his father's sins.

"It is wrong for Father to do this and not obey God," he often whispered to himself, making sure no one could hear him. "It isn't because Father doesn't know the law. Everyone knows the law." He sighed, thinking back on all he had been taught.

Many years before Josiah or Amon was born, God had given Moses rules for the people of Israel. The rules were written on flat rocks called tablets. One rule was that the Lord God was the only God they should worship. They were not to make idols or bow down and serve them. Yet King Amon had many ugly idols in his house. Josiah hated them. When he was very small, he made faces and stuck out his tongue at them when he passed by. As he grew older, he refused to look at them at all. *If only Father would throw them all away and obey God!*

One day some of Amon's servants rose up and killed the king. This made the people of the land so angry that they killed all the servants who had conspired against Amon. They also insisted on crowning Josiah as their king!

"How can I rule the people?" Josiah said in despair. "I am only eight years old!"

God knew that Josiah loved Him and had always tried to do right. He was pleased, and He helped Josiah be a good king.

Josiah served God all the days of his life. The "boy king" ruled in Jerusalem for thirty-one years. He went to the house of the Lord, and all the men of Judah and all the inhabitants of Jerusalem went with him, including the priests and the prophets. Josiah read to them the Book of the Law that had been found in the temple. Standing by a pillar, he made a covenant with the Lord to follow His teachings. All the people pledged to do the same.

"Bring the vessels and everything that has to do with Baal and all the other false gods out of the temple of the Lord and from the grove," Josiah ordered. "They are to be burned outside of Jerusalem in the fields of the Kidron Valley."

The priests did as commanded. The "boy king" had abolished idolatry.

2 Kings 21–22

ezra and nehemiah rebuild jerusalem

Ezra and Nehemiah emerged during a pivotal time in Jewish history. After decades of captivity in Babylon, they led many people back to Judah to rebuild Jerusalem and its temple both structurally and spiritually.

Ezra, a priest and scholar versed in God's law, was a descendant of Aaron, the first high priest. He was in charge of some of the returning exiles. A wonderfully devout man, Ezra led his flock in prayer and fasting. His role was to end the practice of Jews marrying non-Jews from neighboring countries and to return the people to God's ordained pattern of worship.

Meanwhile, Nehemiah was still living in Persia, where he served as the emperor's wine steward. Nehemiah learned of the difficulties the Jews were encountering in Jerusalem. They lived in fear of surrounding nations, and the protective wall around Jerusalem was in ruins. The Persian emperor granted him permission to go to Jerusalem and supervise the rebuilding of the city's wall. In fact, God so stirred the emperor's heart that Nehemiah was given an escort and building materials.

As the Israelites worked on the wall, their enemies plotted against them. God repeatedly thwarted these plots. Nehemiah prayed often and calmed his people's fears by organizing the workers: Half of them, fully armed, stood guard while the other half toiled at the wall. Even the wall builders carried swords.

When the wall was finished, it was obvious to both the Israelites and their enemies that God's hand had been upon its building. The people asked Ezra to read the law to them; then they prayed, confessed their sins and the sins of their ancestors, and signed an agreement to live in obedience to God.

God's work is often fraught with danger and uncertainty. During the period of the restoration of Jerusalem, the Israelites could not rest easy. Their leaders had to be alert and live in close contact with God. Ezra and Nehemiah rose to this demand.

Ezra 7–10:17; Nehemiah

hadassah, queen of persia

Hadassah, also known as Esther, "the star," had neither father nor mother but dwelled in the house of her cousin Mordecai, who treated her as a daughter. They were of the captive nation of Judah and living in Persia. One day Mordecai said, "The king has sent a decree throughout the land. All wives are to give honor to their husbands. Queen Vashti refused to come at the king's command when his heart was merry with much wine. She has been banished."

Esther felt a tiny pulse beat in her throat.

"All the fair young virgins are to be gathered unto Shushan the palace, to the house of the women. The maiden who pleases the king shall be queen instead of Vashti. Esther, think what it would mean should you be chosen."

A flush went over the beautiful face. As queen, she could help her people.

"Do not tell the king you are Jewish," Mordecai warned.

After twelve months of purification rites, Esther went to the king. She so found favor with him that Ahasuerus loved Esther above all the women. He set the royal crown on her head and made her queen instead of Vashti.

Mordecai, who often stood outside the palace gate to hear news of his cousin, learned that two of the king's chamberlains who kept the door planned to lay hands on Ahasuerus. He told Esther, who informed the king. The culprits were hanged and the deed written in the king's chronicles.

Haman, a courtier set above all the princes of the kingdom, hated Mordecai. The Jew would not bow to him. Haman told lies to the king about the Jews and convinced him that the Jewish men, women, and children should be destroyed on a certain day.

Mordecai donned sackcloth and ashes. When Esther sent to know why, he told her of the king's command. He warned that even she could not escape. She sent back and asked all Jews to fast for her. On the third day, she went and stood in the court. She prayed the king would extend his scepter to her. If he did not, she could die for daring to approach him. The king summoned her forward.

Esther invited both him and Haman to a banquet. Once they were there, she made a petition, inviting them to a second banquet the next day. That night the king, unable to sleep, read his chronicles and discovered the service Mordecai had done for him. He also realized Mordecai had never received a reward. The next day, he asked Haman what honor a loyal man should receive. Haman named great things, thinking it would all be for him. . .then had to see it all bestowed on Mordecai.

At the second banquet that night, Esther courageously exposed Haman's plot. She confessed that she also was Jewish and subject to the decree.

The king immediately hanged Haman on a gallows he had constructed for Mordecai and gave Mordecai Haman's house and his own royal ring. Yet he had no power to reverse the order he had given concerning the slaughter of the Jews, for it had been written and sealed with the king's ring. All he could do was grant the Jews in every part of the land permission to defend themselves.

This he did. He also sent Mordecai out from his presence arrayed in royal apparel and with a great crown of gold. The Jews rejoiced.

No enemy could withstand the fierce fighting of the Jews, once given a decree to defend themselves. Fair and lovely Esther's bravery saved not only her life, but the lives of her people. Her story stands today as an example of one who fearlessly took chances and did all she could to right the wrongs done her people, even when her actions could have led to her own death.

Esther 1–10

job, man with an upright heart

"You have the patience of Job."

Smile if someone pays you that compliment, because Job was one of the most honorable characters in the Bible. He was a wealthy man whose family, fortune, health, and friendships were suddenly taken from him for no apparent reason. Yet he refused to succumb to unbelief. Though he lamented aloud, Job knew his Lord had a reason for his predicament, and he patiently waited for things to be made right.

Job lived in the land of Uz and was a faithful believer in

God. In fact, God told Satan that Job was the most faithful man in the world.

"The only reason he worships You," Satan retorted, "is that You protect him and bless everything he does. How do You think he would behave if You let him lose all he has? He'll curse You."

"We'll see," God said and let Job's wonderful world collapse around him.

Afterward, Job was visited by three friends, Eliphaz, Bildad, and Zophar. They came to comfort him, but they were hardly a comfort to this godly man. They did not understand Job's devout faith. It seemed apparent to them that Job was being punished because he had done something wrong.

Job knew better. He was not perfect, but he certainly had not committed enough sins to warrant the intensity of sufferings he had been given. Although he demanded to know why God had let him fall into such a state and even became very angry with God, Job never lost faith.

God's reply was a stern and eloquent reminder of His incredible power and the insignificance of human understanding. Job apologized for questioning the Lord's decisions. Then God turned His reproach on the three friends for misinterpreting the meaning of Job's plight. In the end, God made Job twice as wealthy as before.

When we see good people around us afflicted with terrible diseases, tragedies, and setbacks, we should remember Job, who lost everything but his understanding of God's faithfulness.

Job

the ideal woman

In a male-dominated world where only the most outstanding (or notorious!) women received much attention, Solomon offers a glowing portrait of the ideal woman. His tribute also elevates everyday tasks and describes the value of those who strive to live up to their God-given womanhood.

Although written to those who lived long ago, much of Proverbs 31:10–31 remains applicable today. The New International Version of the Bible aptly titles this section of scripture "The Wife of Noble Character."

A wife of noble character who can find?
  She is worth far more than rubies.
Her husband has full confidence in her
  and lacks nothing of value.
She brings him good, not harm,
  all the days of her life.
She selects wool and flax
  and works with eager hands.
She is like the merchant ships,
  bringing her food from afar.
She gets up while it is still dark;
  she provides food for her family
  and portions for her servant girls.
She considers a field and buys it;
  out of her earnings she plants a vineyard.
She sets about her work vigorously;
  her arms are strong for her tasks.
She sees that her trading is profitable,
  and her lamp does not go out at night.
In her hand she holds the distaff
  and grasps the spindle with her fingers.
She opens her arms to the poor
  and extends her hands to the needy.
When it snows, she has no fear for her household;
  for all of them are clothed in scarlet.
She makes coverings for her bed;
  she is clothed in fine linen and purple.
Her husband is respected at the city gate,
  where he takes his seat among the elders of the land.

She makes linen garments and sells them,
and supplies the merchants with sashes.
She is clothed with strength and dignity;
she can laugh at the days to come.
She speaks with wisdom,
and faithful instruction is on her tongue.
She watches over the affairs of her household
and does not eat the bread of idleness.
Her children arise and call her blessed;
her husband also, and he praises her:
"Many women do noble things,
but you surpass them all."
Charm is deceptive, and beauty is fleeting;
but a woman who fears the LORD is to be praised.
Give her the reward she has earned,
and let her works bring her praise at the city gate.

Proverbs 31

isaiah, spokesman of God

Isaiah is one of the best-known Hebrew prophets. He spoke for God in Jerusalem during the eighth century BC at the time when Assyria conquered Israel and carried many victims into exile.

According to Isaiah's own description, he was a Jew "of unclean lips" living in an unclean nation. In a vision he saw the Lord sitting on a throne attended by winged seraphs. One of the seraphs took a live coal from the Lord's altar, flew down, and touched Isaiah's lips with the coal. "Now your record has been blotted clean, and you no longer are guilty," the angel told him.

The Lord needed a spokesman to show the Israelites their sins and turn them back to His ways. "Whom shall I send?" God asked.

"Here I am," responded the awestruck Isaiah. "Send me."

Isaiah prophesied for forty years during the reigns of four kings. He knew the Israelites had much more to fear from their own wrongdoing and lack of faith than they did from the Assyrians. He preached to Israel before and after their captivity. He reminded them of God's faithfulness to their ancestors and taught them that God is in control of all history.

"Do you think I have divorced you like a man divorces his wife?" God asked the downtrodden Israelites through His prophet. "Then where are the divorce papers?" God still loved His people, Isaiah proclaimed, and would rescue them. He said that the Lord was building a new creation, a place of peace, where there would be no sorrow or death. "Therefore, rejoice!" Isaiah exhorted.

Throughout his prophecies, Isaiah foretells the coming of the Messiah, a descendant of Jesse, a cornerstone, shepherd, and bearer of salvation. With good reason Isaiah cried, "Rejoice!"

Isaiah

jeremiah, youthful prophet

If you think you're too young or too ordinary to be used by God, consider Jeremiah. He was probably still in his teens when God called him to prophesy in Judah. Jeremiah thought he was too young and not a particularly good speaker. But the Lord would have none of these protests. "Go where I tell you to go," God commanded. "Do not be afraid; I'll be with you." He touched Jeremiah's mouth and told him, "I have put My words in your mouth."

The Lord sent Jeremiah to Jerusalem, where the prophet delivered God's indictment to the sinful, idolatrous people. He pointed out their unfaithfulness and that of their ancestors. He asked them to return to God. He repeatedly warned of invasion from the north: Jerusalem was about to be devastated. Jeremiah went so far as to tell the Israelites to surrender to the Babylonians rather than die in battle.

The people were not happy to hear this message, especially coming from one so young. But Jeremiah also preached that the Lord would rescue the Israelites and rebuild their nation after they returned to Him. But that did not mollify the people's anger. The Jews plotted to kill Jeremiah and actually threw him in prison for his preaching.

More than any other prophet, Jeremiah revealed his own disgruntlement and questions. "You told us we would have peace, but a sword is at our throats," he whined to God. He personally agonized as he told the people of their coming defeat. When they laughed at him, he expressed his anger openly.

Perhaps because of his youth, Jeremiah held nothing back. But he was spiritually mature. This is seen in his prayer, "I know we humans are not in control. Punish me as I deserve—but not in anger, for that would kill me." Jeremiah reminds us that God is in control of every situation.

_____

Jeremiah

ezekiel's visions

Dem bones, dem bones, dem dry bones. . .
Dem bones gonna rise again. . . .

Apart from the African-American spirituals we have sung for generations, most Christians have only a sketchy acquaintance with the prophet Ezekiel.

Ezekiel prophesied in the sixth century BC just before Jerusalem's fall and as the Jews were exiled into Babylon. He had a singular encounter with the Lord, who showed him an astounding vision: Four living creatures, each with four wings, appeared within a shining windstorm; each creature had four faces, one of a human, a lion, a bull, and an eagle; beside each creature was a bright wheel within a wheel with eyes around the rims. At length Ezekiel realized he was witnessing a form of the Lord's glory. In this way God appointed Ezekiel to prophesy to the Israelites.

Early in his book, Ezekiel warned the people of Judah that their sins would bring about the ruination of Jerusalem. He predicted the captivity of the Jews and urged the people to return to the Lord's ways. Ultimately he described Jerusalem as a worthless vine that needed to be punished and put to shame. He also predicted God's judgment against rival nations: Ammon, Moab, Edom, Philistia, Tyre, and Egypt.

A most memorable part of Ezekiel's prophecy is his vision of the nation of Israel as dry bones lying in a valley. God promised that He would free these dead, hopeless bones from their entombment and cause them to live again.

Ezekiel foretold the restoration of Jerusalem and described in detail how the temple would be rebuilt. He explained the way worship would be conducted in that new temple and how the land would be subdivided among the Israelites upon their return. His prophecy covers the concerns of the captive people with warnings, encouragement, and assurances that they would in time regain their lost kingdom.

Ezekiel

daniel, captive prophet

From the time of his youth, it was obvious Daniel was to be used by the Lord for important work. Then the Babylonians captured Jerusalem. Still, Daniel and three of his friends were outstanding among the Hebrew captives because of their youth, intelligence, handsome appearance, and strength. Therefore, they were selected to be trained for service in King Nebuchadnezzar's court.

But Daniel—who had been given the Babylonian name Belteshazzar—demonstrated his determination to live in the godly way in which he had been raised, even if it meant jeopardizing his favored standing among his captors. Nebuchadnezzar ordered that the trainees be given royal food and drink, thinking it would maximize their strength and wit as they grew. But the food was unacceptable according to Jewish custom. Daniel asked his guard to give him and his three friends only vegetables and water.

"What if you end up looking paler than the other captives?" the guard said. "Then I'll be killed for disobeying the king's orders."

"Try it for ten days," Daniel suggested. "Then compare us with the other young men."

Not only did they pass the test; their austere, clean diet made them healthier than the others.

After three years of training, all the young men were interviewed by King Nebuchadnezzar. Daniel and his three friends far surpassed the others in every skill. So the king appointed them to important court positions and relied on their wisdom when he needed advice.

Daniel was particularly wise and had the God-given power to interpret dreams, as well. This earned him the king's deepest respect; Daniel was made a governor and named chief counselor. But Daniel made it clear that his abilities did not imply he was in any way superior to any of the other advisors. Rather, he said, God simply had chosen to use him to explain certain things.

Daniel and his friends—whom the Babylonians had named Shadrach, Meshach, and Abednego—were faithful to God in the face of their captors' idol worship. On one occasion, Shadrach, Meshach, and Abednego were thrown into a furnace for refusing to worship a towering gold statue erected near the city. The heat of the furnace was so intense that it killed the men who guarded it, while its intended victims, accompanied by an angel, walked unhurt in the fire. King Nebuchadnezzar was so impressed that he had to respect their God. In time, he himself came to believe in God.

Daniel served under Nebuchadnezzar, his son Belshazzar, King Darius, and later King Cyrus of Persia, and won the highest respect of each of them. It was Belshazzar who commanded that Daniel interpret the mysterious handwriting that appeared on the wall of the king's banquet hall. The message, Daniel accurately interpreted, foretold the end of Belshazzar's reign.

During Darius's reign, governors and officials who were jealous of Daniel's wisdom and power contrived to have the king issue a decree forbidding anyone in the kingdom to pray to any god—on pain of death! Naturally, Daniel continued to pray daily. This was reported to Darius. He was horrified, because to uphold his decree he would have to order the execution of Daniel, his most trusted advisor. Reluctantly he had Daniel cast into a den of lions and then prayed himself that God would save his servant.

And God did so by sending an angel to keep the lions at bay throughout the night. In the morning Darius ordered Daniel released and his accusers thrown to the lions. Then the king ordered everyone in his kingdom to worship Daniel's God, whom Darius recognized as the one true God.

Daniel

nebuchadnezzar, babylonian king

It took a lot of convincing for King Nebuchadnezzar of Babylon to decide to worship God. He reigned during the sixth and seventh centuries BC at the time Jerusalem was captured. Daniel and his colleagues, carried into captivity by the Babylonian army, were trained for royal service. In time, they were given important managerial positions under Nebuchadnezzar. Daniel in particular became indispensable to the king because he was able to interpret Nebuchadnezzar's strange dreams. The king respected Daniel and the others, but he gave little thought to their God.

When Shadrach, Meshach, and Abednego refused to worship Nebuchadnezzar's golden idol, he had them thrown into a fiery furnace. They survived and emerged unsinged, as if nothing had happened. The king was amazed and promoted them to more powerful positions, but still he declined to worship their God.

But the Lord in His kindness reached out to Nebuchadnezzar. As He often does, God used affliction to draw the king to Him. God took away Nebuchadnezzar's kingdom and power for seven years. Nebuchadnezzar later described himself as living like a wild animal during that time. Some students of scripture believe this was a result of a hallucination or mental derangement. Whatever the condition, Nebuchadnezzar at last prayed to Daniel's God. He was healed and restored to power.

Nebuchadnezzar gave this testimony of praise: "Glorify the King in heaven, for He is truthful and fair, and He humiliates the proud." Clearly, God had struck a nerve in Nebuchadnezzar when he demonstrated that He was Lord even over that which matters most to a king—his royal pride.

Daniel 1–4

hosea, cheated husband

The unfaithful wife deserted her husband for a lover. The husband paid for her return to his household! This, the story of the prophet Hosea, parallels the message he brought to the people of Israel. Israel had betrayed their Lord like a promiscuous wife, yet

God in His mercy was willing to buy them back!

Hosea could understand the agonizing relationship between God and His wayward people better than any other prophet, because he knew similar agony in his own life. He could speak to the Israelites bluntly and harshly but with genuine underlying love. He knew of the pain they were causing their Maker by their long history of disobedience. And God's pain was heightened by the fact that He loved them passionately.

Hosea's prophecy contained a straightforward accusation against the people's sins and idolatry. "Judgment is coming," he warned. "Bondage will follow. You have trusted in your own power, so you will reap destruction."

But near the end of his book, Hosea poignantly conveyed God's irrevocable love for His people. "How can I give you up?" God said. "I am not man; I am God, and I love you tenderly. I will not vent My wrath on you." Hosea concludes with a plea for Israel to repent and a final assurance of God's forgiveness if the people would only turn back to Him.

Hosea

joel and the locusts

Locusts!

The plague that swept through Israel around the fifth century BC was one of the most dramatic in Old Testament history. God used it to punish His sinful people, and through the prophet Joel promised His forgiveness if they changed their ways.

Joel likened the locusts to a hostile army, a nation, and "a people great and strong." Far too many to be counted, the locusts were laying waste the land of Israel, which once had been as fruitful as the Garden of Eden. These locusts got Israel's attention, and then Joel sounded the alarm. Hopefully the

Israelites would listen to his warning of judgment day.

Joel prophesied that when Israel repented, God would bless them again by sending His Holy Spirit. Their enemies would be punished and the faithful would be saved. He spoke of the day of judgment when the sun would be darkened, the moon would be turned to blood, and enemy nations would lie desolate. But God's people would find refuge in a land where "the mountains. . .drip new wine and the hills. . .flow with milk."

Joel's is a prophecy of stark contrasts—light and darkness, good and evil, struggles in punishment, and rest in God's presence.

Joel

---

amos, farmer-prophet

"The Lord will roar from Zion. . . ."

So begins the prophecy of Amos, a sheep breeder and keeper of fig trees in Tekoa, a town in the land of Judah. God told him to leave this work and preach to the people of Bethel in Israel. Amos obeyed.

His message was indeed a roar. Amos began by proclaiming the Lord's judgment against the neighboring nations of Syria, Philistia, Phoenicia, Edom, Ammon, Moab, and Judah. He then declared God's wrath against Israel for a long litany of offenses. Amos particularly cited the rich who mistreated the poor and those who worshiped lifeless idols.

"Return to Me and you will live," he told the Israelites. Amos promised a coming day of doom but concluded with the Lord's pledge to rebuild the fallen kingdom.

Amos is among the twelve minor prophets of the Old Testament and was the first biblical writer to teach that God rules the entire universe.

Amos

Storms on the Mediterranean Sea can be fearful, and none was more ominous than the one that boiled there in 862 BC and engulfed a little ship outbound from Joppa.

The vessel rocked dangerously and was deluged by wave after great wave while the crew tossed cargo overboard to lighten the load. They also prayed fervently. But the storm intensified.

They thought that perhaps someone among them had provoked the Lord's wrath and brought on this calamity. Then they remembered the passenger Jonah. They knew he was fleeing from God. Yet he was fast asleep despite the drastic pitching of the vessel. Who was he? What had he done to bring on such terror?

Jonah admitted he was the likely cause of their peril. And he told the crew the solution—throw him into the sea, then the waters would calm. The sailors at first could not bring themselves to do this. They tried to maneuver the ship toward land, but it was futile. So they followed Jonah's brazen advice and cast him into the sea. Immediately the storm abated.

Jonah was a Hebrew prophet. The Lord had commanded that he travel to Nineveh, a huge city on the river Tigris far to the northeast of Judea. There he was to warn the people that their wickedness would soon be punished. It seemed to Jonah that this was a long way to go for nothing but trouble. So he fled by ship in the opposite direction. Jonah wanted the Lord to find another prophet for His difficult and dangerous mission to Nineveh.

Despite Jonah's attempt to flee from God, his disobedience was used for God's purposes. The experience of the storm and the sudden calming of the waves was such a dramatic demonstration of the Lord's power and grace that the crew of the ship worshiped God and pledged to honor Him.

Meanwhile, God had no intention of letting Jonah off the hook—even by death. So a gigantic fish swallowed the hapless man after he was cast from the ship. For three days the fish swam the sea with Jonah alive in its belly. The wretched prophet prayed for his life and repented, and the Lord heard. At God's command, the leviathan vomited Jonah onto the shore.

Jonah followed God's orders, journeyed to Nineveh, and preached to the people that because of their sinfulness, their city would be destroyed in forty days. The people listened, stopped their evil ways, and asked the Lord's forgiveness. The Lord forgave them and granted their city a reprieve from judgment.

However, instead of being overjoyed at the Ninevites' change of heart, Jonah was angry. God had sent him on this exhausting, dangerous errand, knowing full well that in the end the people would repent and be forgiven! "I want to die," the pitiful Jonah told the Lord. "You care about the wrong things," said the Lord. "It is right for Me to be concerned for a great city like Nineveh."

Jonah

zechariah, messianic prophet

Rejoice, Jerusalem!
Shout, Jerusalem!
Your King is coming.
He is righteous, and He brings salvation.
He is gentle, and He rides on the foal of a donkey. . . .

Thus Zechariah predicted the coming of Jesus Christ more than five hundred years before His birth. The Jews had returned from captivity in Babylon and began rebuilding the temple and the city of Jerusalem. Zechariah spoke not only of their labors in Jerusalem but of things to come as well. These include the punishment of Israel's ungodly leaders and of the nation's enemies, the coming of the Messiah, the people's repentance from their idolatrous ways, the Lord's final victory over His enemies, and the millennial kingdom.

Jesus Himself referred to Zechariah's prophecy during the Last Supper. "Tonight," He told His disciples, "all of you will stumble because of Me." Then He quoted Zechariah: "Kill the Shepherd and the sheep will scatter."

Zechariah's prophecies serve as stern, necessary warnings to wayward people. They are also words of hope and vital connectors from Old Testament history to Jesus Christ and to the building of His glorious church.

Zechariah; Matthew 26:31

matthew, tax collector turned apostle

A Jewish tax collector was not a desirable companion in first-century Palestine, where the Jews lived under bondage to Roman taxes. Yet Matthew was called by Jesus and joined His band of disciples. When the Pharisees demanded to know why Jesus associated with "sinners and tax collectors," Jesus replied, "Those who are well do not need a doctor. I've come to call sinners, not righteous people, to repent."

Matthew wrote an in-depth account of Jesus' life and teachings. Whereas Luke wanted to reach Gentile readers with the good news of Jesus' salvation, Matthew's objective was to convince Jews that Jesus was the Messiah as foretold in the Old Testament.

Matthew's record provides the most thorough version of the Sermon on the Mount. He emphasized Jesus' concern with righteousness and concluded with the commission Jesus gave the disciples just before He ascended into heaven: "Go, make disciples in all the nations. . . ."

Little is known of Matthew's life. Varying accounts say he

died in Ethiopia or Macedonia, possibly of natural causes, possibly by execution.

Matthew; Mark 2:13–17; 3:13–19; Luke 5:27–32; 6:12–16; Acts 1:12–14

mary and joseph, family of Christ

Clip-clopping hooves of a little donkey chosen more for strength than beauty sent spirals up from the dusty road two travelers plodded. Mary shifted in a vain attempt to find a more comfortable position. "I pray we shall reach Bethlehem soon," she told the sturdy man who walked beside her.

"It is not far now," he encouraged. A slight frown wrinkled his sweaty forehead. "Is it well with thee and thy babe?" He anxiously glanced at her cumbersome body, great with child.

"It is well." She smiled at her husband and smothered a small, secret sigh. The journey from Nazareth had been long and hard. Swarms of people crowded the roads and made traveling difficult. Rich and poor, in health and sickness, old and young, all sought their birthplace to be counted and taxed, for the decree of Caesar Augustus exempted no one.

The little donkey plodded on, one ear drooping. Mary rested against the rolled blankets Joseph had thoughtfully strapped on the donkey and the strong hand he placed against her back. Weariness swept over her like waves on the Sea of Galilee, blurring the present, recalling the past. . . .

Mary slowly opened her eyes. Had someone called? Nay. Quiet lay over the room like a shimmering veil. And yet. . .

"Hail, thou that art highly favored; the Lord is with thee. blessed art thou among women." A glowing figure stood beside her.

Mary shrank in terror. *What manner of salutation might this be?*

The angel—for such he must be—said, "Fear not, Mary. For thou hast found favor with God. And behold, thou shalt conceive in thy womb, and bring forth a son, and shalt call His name Jesus. He shall be great and shall be called the Son of the Highest, and the Lord God shall give unto Him the throne of His father David. And He shall reign over the house of Jacob forever, and of His kingdom there shall be no end."

She, bear a child? Although she was espoused to Joseph the carpenter, they had not yet become man and wife. "How shall this be, seeing I know not a man?" Mary asked, unable to tear her gaze from the shining figure.

The angel replied, "The Holy Ghost shall come upon thee, and the power of the Highest shall overshadow thee. Therefore also that holy thing which shall be born of thee shall be called the Son of God." He went on to tell her, "Behold, thy cousin Elisabeth, she hath also conceived a son in her old age, and this is the sixth month with her, who was called barren. For with God nothing shall be impossible." Truth radiated in every word.

Belief and acceptance stirred in Mary's heart. The Lord God of Israel who created the earth and the heavens, who parted the sea and fed His children in the wilderness, possessed power that knew no bounds. "Behold the handmaid of the Lord; be it unto me according to thy word," Mary whispered. Joy and trembling filled her soul, and she bowed in humility. When she raised her head, the angel had departed from her.

After a time of pondering all the things the angel had said, Mary knew what she must do. "I will arise and go to Elisabeth," she decided. So began a time of newness for the Jewish maiden. Her visit with Elisabeth confirmed the truth of all she had been told, yet a great wall rose in Mary's life. Could Joseph, loving and kind as he was, believe what had come upon her? Or would he think her a bad woman, one who sought to cover her sins with wild tales?

In fear and trembling, Mary related all the angel had said. She saw the shock in Joseph's eyes, the pain and disappointment that one he had thought pure should come to this sad state.

Should he make her a public example, she would be stoned. What, then, would become of the babe she carried, the child the angel said was the Son of God?

A just man who loved Mary with all his heart, Joseph considered the matter day and night. He was minded to put her away privately, for he could not bear to see her stoned, even if she had sinned against heaven and against him.

While he thought on these things, the angel of the Lord appeared to him in a dream. "Joseph. . .fear not to take unto thee Mary thy wife, for that which is conceived in her is of the Holy Ghost."

The angel spoke other things, confirming Mary's story, then departed. Joseph rose from his sleep. He wanted to climb to the rooftops and shout to any who might listen, "She is innocent! My Mary is pure and chosen among all women to bear a son who shall be called Emmanuel, 'God with us.' " When he told Mary all that had come to pass, they rejoiced together.

In the months that followed, Mary found herself in a strange state. She hugged knowledge to her heart and marveled. Sometimes her heart beat until she thought it might burst. Why had she, of all the virgins in Nazareth, nay, in the entire land, been chosen to bear the Son of God? She thought of other maidens, older and more experienced than she, worthy and devoted. Would she be able to succor and care for the child in the proper way? Yet each time doubts came, the razor-sharp memory of the angel's visit, the words that had burned into her heart, rose to reassure her. And each time, she bowed herself and humbly prayed she might be worthy of the great honor and responsibility to which she had been called. . . .

"Mary." A gentle hand pressed her shoulder. She returned from her remembrances. "We have reached Bethlehem."

A sharp pain tore through her. "It is a good thing," she gasped and laced her fingers together over her swollen belly.

"Hasten, little friend," Joseph told the donkey, who obligingly broke into a faster pace. Yet as the three travelers went from inn to inn and found no place, Mary fought ever-increasing pain.

At last a kindly innkeeper offered them a place in a dry, warm cave where he kept his animals. By then Mary little cared for anything except a place to rest and deliver her child. What mattered it whether He be born in inn or stable? She must have shelter and soon.

Before the cock crowed, Mary brought forth her firstborn son. She wrapped Him in swaddling clothes and laid Him in a manger. Spent, she held Him close, sensing the present moment might be the most precious of her life. A little later, she roused to voices. Shepherds knelt before her, faces working, eyes turned toward the babe. They told her angels had proclaimed the baby's birth while they were in the fields keeping their sheep. They glorified God and praised Him. Mary tucked their visit away in her heart to be pondered later.

From glory to agony, from childbearing through Jesus' childhood to the cross and beyond, Mary, mother of Jesus, is history's finest reminder that with God, nothing shall be impossible.

Matthew 1; Luke 1–2

Jesus Christ, Son of God

For the prophets He is the Messiah.
For Mary He is a son.
For God He is the Son.
For Herod He is a threat.
For the wise men He is the King of the Jews.
For the shepherds He is heralded by angels.
For Simeon He is the consolation of Israel.
For the religious leaders He is a challenger.
For His fellow Nazarenes He is an outcast.
For the demon-possessed He is the liberator.
For the blind He is the giver of sight.

For the lame He is the transformer.
For the dead He is the reviver.
For the hungry multitude He is the provider.
For the children He is the defender.
For sinners He is forgiveness.
For the ignorant He is the teacher.
For the storm-tossed He walks on water.
For the diseased He is the healer.
For lost sheep He is the shepherd.
For the sins of the world He is the Lamb of God.
For Thomas He is an enigma.
For Judas Iscariot He is a profit source.
For Pontius Pilate He is an annoyance.
For witnesses of the crucifixion He is an object of contempt.
And for all who receive Him, who believe in His name,
He gives power to become children of God.

How could the people of the first century believe that the Messiah had at long last arrived? Jesus Christ was certainly not what they expected. He did not act like a king, or even a priest. He selected commoners, even sinners, for companions and loved the poor, the rich, the young, the old, the Jew, the Gentile, the persecutor, and the persecuted. There was no one He did not love.

There is no one Jesus Christ does not love. He receives all who come to Him and can be reached instantly by anyone from anywhere. One can never intrude upon Jesus. He waits to hear from you!

john the baptist, forerunner of Christ

"Prepare the way of the Lord!"

This was the task of John the Baptist, son of Zacharias and

Elisabeth. He was a powerful preacher in the Judean desert who wore camel skin clothes and ate a diet of locusts and wild honey. People came to John in great numbers, and he admonished them to repent and confess their sins, whereupon he baptized them in the river Jordan. They asked him if he was the Messiah, to which he replied, "No." But soon the Messiah would appear and would baptize not with water but with the Holy Spirit.

One day John's cousin Jesus came to be baptized. This, John knew, was the man whose arrival he had predicted. "You should baptize me instead," John protested.

But Jesus reassured him, "This is the way God wants us to do it."

So John baptized Jesus in the river. When the Lord emerged from the water, the Holy Spirit came down from the sky and descended upon Jesus like a dove. A voice from heaven proclaimed, "This is my beloved Son. I am well pleased with Him." Thus began Jesus' ministry.

Shortly afterward, John was thrown into prison by King Herod. This occurred because Herodias, Herod's wife, was angry that John had denounced their marriage. She had previously been Herod's brother's wife, and John told Herod that he was wrong to take his brother's wife. Herodias wanted John killed, but Herod, who feared John's popularity, preserved the prophet's life and merely imprisoned him.

John was unsettled by doubt while in prison and sent this message to Jesus: "Are You really the Messiah?"

"Tell John what you are seeing and hearing," Jesus told John's disciples. "The blind see, the lame walk, those with leprosy are healed, the deaf hear, the dead are raised up, and the poor receive the news of salvation. God will bless those who do not reject Me."

This reassurance came at a critical time, because Herodias soon found a way to end John's life. Herodias's daughter danced for Herod and his guests at a birthday celebration. The king was so captivated by this that in a moment of weakness he promised her anything she desired. Prompted by her mother, the girl demanded, "Bring me the head of John the Baptist."

Herod was shocked and distraught, but he could not go back on his promise. So the great John the Baptist, forerunner of Jesus Christ, was beheaded to appease a sinful queen.

John's epitaph is Jesus' own words: "What did you go out into the desert to see? . . . A man dressed in fine clothes? No, those who wear fine clothes are in kings' palaces. Then what did you go out to see? A prophet? Yes, I tell you, and more than a prophet. . . . Among those born of women there has not risen anyone greater than John the Baptist."

Matthew 3; 4:12; 11:2–19; Mark 1:1–11; 6:14–29; Luke 1; 3:1–22; 9:7–9; John 1:19–37

john the apostle

John and his brother James followed in the footsteps of their father, Zebedee, and became fishermen. Their friends, the brothers Andrew and Peter, were also fishermen. All four were called to be His disciples by Christ early in His ministry.

In the Gospel, John gave us firsthand accounts of many of the Savior's miracles, beginning with the wedding at Cana where Jesus turned the water into wine, all the way to Jesus' visitations after His resurrection. Although John did not record all the miracles he saw, he offered ample proof that Jesus is the Son of God.

John's Gospel makes effective use of metaphor: In it Jesus is a Shepherd to His flock, the Living Bread and the Water of Life, the Light of the World, and the True Vine. John was a brilliant thinker, an eloquent writer, and passionate in his devotion to the Savior. So much so that from the cross Jesus asked him to care for His mother.

After Jesus' ascension, John labored among the churches

in Asia Minor and is credited with writing Revelation and the epistles of John. Historians believe that of the original twelve disciples, only John died a natural death in his old age.

Matthew 4:21–22; Mark 1:19–20; 10:35–45; John; Acts 3–4; 8:14–17; 1, 2, and 3 John; Revelation

peter, fisher of men

Simon Peter was introduced to Jesus Christ by his brother Andrew. Jesus told the brawny fisherman, "You will be named Cephas," a name that means "stone."

Peter was involved in one of the Savior's first miracles. Jesus had been preaching from Peter's fishing boat to the multitudes gathered along the shore of the Sea of Galilee. When He finished speaking, Jesus told Peter to row into deep water and let down his fishing nets.

"But there are no fish here," Peter complained wearily. "We've been fishing all night, and we've caught nothing."

But he did as Jesus suggested—and caught so many fish that his nets started breaking. His partners came to help, and they pulled up so many fish their boats started to sink.

Awestruck by Jesus' power, Peter fell at His feet. "Stay away from me," Peter told Him. "I'm a terrible sinner."

Jesus already knew this, and it did not affect His plans for Peter. "I'm going to make you a fisher of men," Jesus told him. After Jesus' resurrection and ascension, Peter was a leader of the early church. He was a simple, seemingly impulsive man who did not consider the consequences of his words and deeds.

Peter must have been shaken to his sandals when at the Last Supper Jesus said, "Simon, Satan has asked to sift you like wheat. I have prayed that you will remain faithful." Peter could not imagine what perils Jesus referred to, but he was confident that he would follow the Lord anywhere. "I am even ready to die with you," Peter promised. Jesus corrected him. "Before the rooster crows in the morning, you will deny me three times."

When Jesus was arrested in the garden, Peter tried to defend Him and struck one of the assailants with his sword, cutting off an ear. Jesus admonished Peter to put away his weapon, and with a touch Jesus healed the wounded man. Shortly afterward, Jesus was taken into custody in a house. Peter stayed outside, warming himself near a fire. A servant girl asked, "Weren't you one of His followers?"

"I do not know Him," Peter replied impulsively, fearing for his own safety. Twice more during the next hour, Peter was openly suspected of following Jesus. Both times Peter repeated his denial.

It's sad that the triple denial comes to mind when Peter's name is mentioned, because Peter truly became a stone built into the spiritual house, which is the church of God.

Matthew; Mark; Luke; John; Acts 1–5, 9–12; 1 Peter; 2 Peter

Jesus heals lepers

Of all the miracles of healing Jesus performed, none impressed those who followed Him as much as when He healed lepers. Lepers were outcasts, feared by the people and forced to live in caves or other places away from everyone else. No one wanted to be around them, for fear of catching their loathsome disease. Those with the disease were forced to call out, "Unclean! Unclean!" to announce their presence when they came near others.

Jesus loved the lepers as much as He loved anyone else. He had compassion on those who were shunned. He, too, was often mistreated, and His heart ached for all of God's children who were persecuted.

One day when Jesus came down from the mountain where He had been teaching many things to those who came to listen, great multitudes followed Him.

Suddenly the cry of a leper rose above the noise of the crowd. "Unclean! Unclean!"

The people parted one from another, even as the Red Sea had parted centuries before and provided a way for the children of Israel to escape Pharaoh's armies. Angry shouts arose. How dare a leper boldly thrust himself among them? He should be punished for endangering the men, women, and children assembled.

Mothers caught their children up in their arms and fled from the fearsome sight of a gaunt, haggard man stumbling toward Jesus. One small girl peeked out from the safety of her mother's shawl. "What is wrong with that man?" she asked. "Why are there white patches on his skin?"

"He is a leper," her mother said, trying to get herself and her child farther away from danger. "The frosty white patches are signs of a disease called leprosy."

The child shuddered. Never had she seen anyone with leprosy. It must be a terrible thing, to make a man look like this.

"Listen, he speaks," someone called.

Silence descended on the scattered crowd like an unexpected rainstorm from a clear blue sky. Everyone present heard the leper's words when he knelt before Jesus and worshiped Him, for he cried out in a voice loud enough to reach the heavens. "Lord, if You are willing, You can make me clean."

The child fixed her gaze on the kneeling figure, then on Jesus. She tugged at her mother's wide sleeve. "Can He, Mother? Can Jesus really do that?"

Her mother held her closer. "I don't know. He has healed many, but to make a leper clean is. . ." Her voice trailed off.

"Look, Mother. Jesus has put out His hand. He is touching the leper."

Her mother gasped. No one willingly touched a leper. Jesus must have gone mad to do such a thing! Yet when He spoke, there was no sign of madness in His ringing words that reached the waiting multitude. "I am willing; be cleansed."

Immediately the man's leprosy was healed. Young as she was, and even from a distance, the little girl's keen eyes could see how healthy skin had replaced the telltale white patches. She could also see Jesus' lips move, but the clamor of the crowd drowned out the words He spoke.

It was later reported that Jesus told the man He had healed to go show himself to the priest, as was the custom, but not to tell anyone else what had happened. The child couldn't understand why Jesus didn't want people to know that He had healed a leper. It seemed to her a wonderful thing. It should be shouted from house to house until everyone knew what Jesus had done.

Matthew 8

a woman of faith

She knelt before Jesus in fear and trembling, an insignificant woman in the midst of a multitude. Desperation and fear had driven her to seek the new prophet, whose wonders were being whispered, shouted, and sung throughout her land. At first she had scoffed. Was not Jesus the son of a Nazarite carpenter?

"Yea," those who spoke to her confirmed. "Yet He is much more."

She considered well whether to present herself to this man of whom she knew nothing except gossip. Would it not be better to go on without hope than to allow herself to believe the teacher might have a cure for the rare blood disease that had plagued her for twelve endless years?

Physician after physician had examined her, sadly shaken their heads, and said they could do nothing. Each time, she died a little more inside. Why such a thing had come upon her, she knew not. Apathy often caused her to ask, "Does it matter?

Soon I must die, and that will be the end."

Memories of a time before the illness destroyed her dreams danced before her. Oh, to once again run free and well through the fields. To walk without weakness, straighten to full height, and move without pain. *It cannot happen if you do not keep seeking a cure,* a voice whispered in her heart.

One evening when she lay sleepless, the woman decided, "I will arise in the morning and seek this Jesus. I will cast myself at His feet. If He is all people say, He will have mercy on me. If not, I die and the pain will be no more." She knew it would require her last measure of strength to travel the short distance to Jesus.

In spite of her determination, in spite of her belief that Jesus was her last and only hope, the stricken woman's heart quailed at the sight of the throng surrounding the One she sought. She felt weakness wash through her as waves wash against the shore during a storm. She could go no farther.

A slight opening in the crowd gave her a glimpse of Jesus. It was enough to renew her. *If I may but touch His garment, I shall be whole,* she said in her heart. She stretched forth her hand. The edge of Jesus' cloak felt rough against her searching fingers. Strength flowed into her. She opened her mouth to cry out she had been healed, but no words came.

Jesus, immediately knowing that virtue had gone out of Him, turned and said, "Who touched my clothes?"

His disciples replied, "You see the multitude thronging around You, yet You ask, 'Who touched Me?' "

But Jesus looked round about to see the woman who had done this thing.

She knelt before him in fear and trembling. "Lord, it was I. I knew if I could but touch the hem of Your garment, I would be healed." Head bowed, she waited. What would He do?

Jesus spoke in a voice like none she had ever heard before. "Daughter, be of good comfort; your faith has made thee whole."

Her faith? Words hung on her shaking lips, the confession of how little faith she had possessed. She looked into Jesus' face, filled with compassion and understanding that swept away any need for explanations.

Tears rained like skies weeping for an unbelieving world. She again bowed her face to the ground, only vaguely aware when the multitude moved on—some following Jesus to ask for blessing; others out of curiosity. Then she stood, praised God, and ran, rejoicing with each breath of air that filled her lungs, every long stride that carried her on her way.

Matthew 9; Mark 5; Luke 8

daughter of jairus, restored to life

Jairus loved his daughter with a love known only to those who have been blessed with one child. When she was stricken with illness, he nearly went mad with grief. She must not die, this child whose twelve short years had blessed his household mightily.

"I will seek out Jesus of Nazareth," he said. "If all the tales of Him are true, He will surely heal my child."

When he reached Jesus, the crowd made way. Was not Jairus one of the rulers of the synagogue? Jairus fell at Jesus' feet, worshiped, and besought Him greatly, saying, "My little daughter lieth at the point of death: I pray Thee, come and lay Thy hands on her, that she may be healed; and she shall live."

Jesus arose and followed Jairus, as did His disciples.

On the way, a disturbance came in the crowd. Jairus seethed with impatience. To one in his daughter's condition, every moment mattered. Why must a tottering woman slow them? The next moment he caught his breath. The woman who barely grazed the hem of Jesus' garment with her fingertips was made whole! Jairus's heart leaped within him. If the Master could heal with only that slight touch, how much more would He do when He laid hands on the child who lay just outside the gates of death?

Jairus's heart sang, then turned to stone when some of his

own household rushed out saying, "Thy daughter is dead: why troublest thou the Master any further?" An unworthy thought crept into his mind and took lodging. Why had Jesus tarried to heal the woman and allowed a child to die? Was the woman's life of more importance than the maiden's?

Did Jesus perceive his thoughts? Perhaps, for He spoke. "Fear not: Believe only, and she shall be made whole."

Jairus stumbled on, torn between the assurance in Jesus' eyes and the utter impossibility of the dead being restored to life. When they at last reached Jairus's home, Jesus permitted only Peter, James, John, Jairus, and his wife to come into the chamber. All the rest wept and bewailed, and when Jesus said, "Weep not; she is not dead, but sleepeth," they laughed Him to scorn.

Jesus ordered them all out. He took the maiden by the hand and said, "Maid, arise."

Her spirit came again, and she arose straightway. And Jesus commanded her parents to give her meat.

Jairus felt faint with astonishment and joy. He saw from his wife's face that she felt the same. When they attempted to thank Jesus, He charged them that they should tell no one what was done. But the fame of Jesus' raising Jairus's daughter went abroad into all that land.

Matthew 9; Mark 5; Luke 8

philip witnesses a miracle

One of the first evangelists on record was the apostle Philip. Soon after he was called by Jesus, he told the skeptic Nathaniel, "We've found the one Moses and the prophets were writing about! He's Jesus of Nazareth."

"Can anything good come out of Nazareth?" Nathaniel grumbled.

There must have been a twinkle in Philip's eye when he replied, "Come and see."

And Nathaniel followed the Lord.

Before miraculously feeding the five thousand at the Sea of Galilee, Jesus likewise must have had a twinkle in His eye when He turned to Philip and asked, "Where can we get enough bread for all these people to eat?"

Philip shook his dead in dismay. "Six months' wage wouldn't buy even a sampling for this many people."

Jesus took all the available food—five loaves of bread and a couple of fish—and turned it into a feast.

Still Philip needed reminding. At the Last Supper, Jesus told His disciples, "No one can come to the Father except through Me."

"Lord, show us the Father," Philip requested. "Then we'll be convinced of what You say."

"Philip, have I been with You all this time, and you still do not know Me?" Jesus answered. "Believe that I am in the Father, and the Father in Me. If you cannot believe My words, then believe because of the miracles you have seen Me perform."

Philip did believe and helped spread the gospel after Jesus' resurrection and ascension. He is thought to have been martyred in Asia Minor.

Matthew 10:1–4; Mark 3:13–19; Luke 6:12–16; John 1:43–51; 6:5–7; 12:20–22; 14:8–14

judas iscariot, greedy disciple

The other apostles never dreamed one of Jesus' twelve closest followers would conspire to turn Him over to His enemies to be falsely accused, tried, and executed.

Judas Iscariot was chosen by Jesus along with the other apostles to go out and preach for Him. He also served as the disciples' treasurer. But he seems to have placed an emphasis on money rather than devotion. When Mary poured perfume upon the Lord, Judas criticized her. "This perfume should have been sold and the money given to the poor," he said. But Jesus respected Mary's gesture and corrected Judas. "The poor will always be with you," Jesus said, "but I will not always be with you."

At the Last Supper, Jesus predicted that one of the twelve who were eating with Him would betray Him. "Surely it can't be me!" cried Judas, although he already had bargained secretly to turn Jesus over to the chief priests for thirty pieces of silver.

"You have said so," Jesus replied.

Later that night, when Jesus went to pray in the Garden of Gethsemane, Judas appeared with a mob. "Rabbi!" greeted Judas, and he kissed his Master. The word *Rabbi* was the code that Judas used to identify Jesus in the darkness.

The mob dragged Jesus away to be tried. But soon Judas heard that Jesus had been given the death sentence. He sorely regretted his betrayal and so took the thirty pieces of silver back to the priests and told them that he had sinned. "Jesus is innocent!" he said. When they refused to listen, Judas threw the money into the temple, went out, and hanged himself.

By law the priests could not put Judas's silver in their treasury—it was blood money. Instead they used it to buy land for a graveyard where nameless strangers could be buried.

Matthew 10:1–4; 26:14–16, 21–25, 45–50; 27:3–10; Mark 3:13–19; 14:10–11, 18–21, 43–45; Luke 6:13–16; 22:3–6, 20–23, 47–48; John 12:1–8; 13:2, 18–30; 17:12; 18:1–5

thomas, doubting apostle

Thomas seems to have been a wet blanket over the joy Jesus spread throughout the land.

When Jesus announced to His disciples they must go to

Bethany where their friend Lazarus had just died, Thomas remarked sarcastically, "Yes, let's all go there and die." At the Last Supper, Jesus assured His apostles He was going to prepare a place for them in the Father's house, and they knew the way to follow Him there. Thomas challenged, "How can we know the way, since we don't even know where You are going?"

And in the aftermath of the crucifixion, when Jesus appeared to His followers, Thomas did not believe their reports of seeing the Master. He would not believe, he vowed, unless he could actually touch the nail-scarred palms and put his hand in the Lord's wounded side. Later Jesus entered the locked room where the disciples were staying, and He showed Thomas the pierced hands and had him feel the wound.

"My Lord and my God!" Thomas cried.

"You believe because you have seen Me," Jesus said. "Blessed are those who believe without seeing."

Thomas joined his colleagues in spreading the good news. Yet still today a skeptic is called a doubting Thomas. But Thomas is an important example to us. All the objective evidence in the world could not convince Thomas that Jesus Christ had risen from the dead. It wasn't enough to be told of the resurrection—not even by his most trusted friends. Thomas had to see Jesus for himself. He had to have a personal encounter with the Savior. And so it has always been for Christ's believers.

Matthew 10:1–4; Mark 3:13–19; Luke 6:12–16; John 11:14–16; 14:1–7; 20:24–29; Acts 1:12–14

james, brother of Jesus

Imagine growing up the brother of Jesus Christ and not knowing that He was the promised Messiah until after the crucifixion and ascension.

James knew how Jesus liked His eggs cooked; how He

reacted after hitting His thumb with a hammer; how He handled incidents of sibling banter and rivalry; His favorite games. As James grew up with Jesus, he did not know that his brother was the incarnate God. Years later he surely remembered the incidents of Jesus' childhood, adolescence, and young manhood with a different understanding.

Some scholars think that James did not become a believer until after Jesus' death and resurrection. Details of his life are few, and learning about him is difficult because the New Testament records four men by the name of James. After Jesus' resurrection, was it his brother James who became head of the first-century church in Jerusalem? Was he the writer of the New Testament letter bearing his name? Some scholars suspect so; others are not sure.

Regardless, envision yourself as Jesus' own brother!

Matthew 13:55; Mark 6:3; Acts 12:17; 15:12–21; 21:18; Galatians 1:19

herod antipas, ruler of galilee

Unscrupulous yet cautious, Herod Antipas ruled Galilee during the lifetime of Jesus Christ. His father, Herod the Great, had been completely heartless when he ordered the cold-blooded killing of every baby boy around Bethlehem in an attempt to eliminate the newborn king of the Jews. Like his father, the younger Herod had no love for Jesus or for John the Baptist. Their ministries were causing an unprecedented sensation throughout the land, but Herod Antipas was not as ruthless as his father. In fact, he tried to avoid the conflict these men would cause him.

Yet Herod Antipas had a particular disdain for John. Herod had taken his brother Philip's wife as his own, and John had boldly pointed out his wrongdoing. The king wanted to arrest and execute John for this, but he was afraid the people would revolt because of their high regard for John.

Then the wife in question, Herodias, forced Herod's hand. She persuaded Herod to have John arrested. Then, using her daughter's sensuous dancing to corrupt his thinking, Herodias obtained an order to have John beheaded. This unnerved the ruler. Not only did he fear the people's reaction, but he privately appreciated John's preaching. But he had promised to do whatever his pretty niece wanted, and at her mother's request, she asked that John be beheaded and his head presented to her on a platter. So it was done.

When Jesus Christ was arrested and dragged before Pilate in Jerusalem, Herod happened to be in the city. Pilate tried to take advantage of this in an effort to shift the role of judge to Herod Antipas. So Pilate sent Jesus and His accusers to Herod. After all, Jesus was a Galilean, so His case came under Herod's authority. Herod was eager to meet Jesus because he wanted to see Him perform a miracle. But Jesus refused to answer Herod's questions. So Herod and his soldiers mocked the prisoner and sent Him back to Pilate.

Scripture says Herod and Pilate, who had been enemies, became friends in the aftermath of Jesus' crucifixion. These two cowardly leaders found a common bond at the turning point of civilization. They may have feared this man from Galilee, but they could not acknowledge the existence of a power above their own or that of Rome.

Matthew 14:1–12; Mark 6:14–29; Luke 23:7–12

herodias, wicked wife of herod

Many were those Herodias, ex-wife of Philip, now married to Philip's brother, hated. Her legendary rages effectively quelled opposition for fear of the retribution she mercilessly dealt out to any who dared speak against her. Yet of all her foes, none loomed larger in her twisted mind than John the Baptizer.

Each time Herodias thought of the wild prophet who had come from the wilderness to thunder and stir up the people, she gnashed her teeth in fury. "How dare he speak against us?" she demanded of Herod, her brother-in-law and husband. "If you do not care that he cries in the streets that you are breaking the law, what about me? Should not the tetrarch have the right to take whatever woman he desires, whether or not she be married to his brother?" She clenched her hands with their painted nails until they became claws, working as if she had her enemy's throat between them and would throttle out John's life.

"Be still," Herod commanded. "You know how powerful John has grown. The multitude who believe in him and count him a prophet daily grows larger." He hesitated and spread his hands in a helpless gesture. "Is it not enough that I had him bound and thrown into prison?"

"Pah! It will never be enough," she retorted. "He has insulted and attempted to shame us before all the people. He must pay with his life. You should have had him executed long since."

"I tell you, I cannot," Herod roared.

Herodias only sneered, secretly despising him for his weakness. If she had the power to order John's death, she would have done so the moment he dared raise his voice and condemn those he should bow down and worship. "Are you then afraid of him?"

"Nay," Herod lied. "But the Baptizer is a just man and holy." He did not add that he had observed John, even heard him gladly, until the prophet publicly denounced him for his adultery.

Herodias said no more at the time. Yet with each passing day, she hated John more and vowed to do him harm in whatever way she could.

Plot after plot came to mind. She would know no peace until John's body lay in the ground and his impudent tongue was forever silenced. Even from his cell, he continued to cry out against her and Herod for their illicit relationship.

Herodias brazenly kept the silken curtains of her litter open when carried through the city streets. She stared into the faces of those she passed, and her wrath against John increased. For although Herod's subjects bowed low in obeisance, their scornful expressions and the epithets hurled at her from the security of the multitude brought flags of scarlet to her vapid, painted face.

"I will bide my time," she vowed. "Then I will strike." Again she curled her sharp-nailed fingers into claws, and anticipation spread over her like honey warmed in the sun.

Matthew 14; Mark 6

salome dances for blood

Salome clasped her hands in delight. "I am really to dance before the court?"

Herodias smiled a curious smile. "Yes, my pet. You must dance as you have never danced before. Much is at stake."

Salome failed to catch any particular significance in her mother's voice. To dance before Herod was great enough honor. To be chosen to perform at the great feast the tetrarch had ordered in honor of his birthday overwhelmed her. Some of her confidence fled. "What if I do not please him?"

Herodias eyed her daughter's beauty, her slim and graceful figure. A gleam came to her calculating gaze. "You shall please him." She tossed her head and laughed. "Herod and the lords, high captains and chief estates of Galilee will be so drunken with wine that a damsel with far fewer charms than you could entertain them. You must do much more, Salome. You are to dance in a way not seen in the court, one that entices and drives men mad at the sight of you. Do you hear?"

A deep flush rose in the girl's smooth cheeks. An uncanny resemblance to the mother who demanded adulation as her due showed in her countenance. "I hear and obey." She half closed her eyes, already planning how she could be more daring, more seductive than all those who had preceded her in Herod's court.

On the great day, Herodias carefully ordered her daughter to remain secluded until time for her dance. She watched and waited, a jeweled spider decked out in royal raiment. Wine flowed like the Jordan in flood. Now came the moment for which Herodias waited. She dared not prolong Salome's entrance much longer, or Herod would be too drunk to fully appreciate the young girl's ravishing dance.

"Now," she beckoned.

Salome burst upon the court in the most sensuous dance ever performed. She saw men's eyes widen with lust for her barely concealed body. She saw Herod's hot gaze fasten itself on her, and she danced on until he called her to him. "Ask of me whatever you will, and I will give it to you." He held his cup for more wine and swore, "Whatever you shall ask of me, I will give it to you, up to half of my kingdom!"

Salome's eyes glistened. Half the kingdom, for her? She opened her mouth to speak, to request jewels, riches beyond belief. Nay, first she must consult with her mother. Much wiser in the ways of the world, Herodias would advise her daughter well.

"What shall I ask?" she demanded of Herodias.

"The head of John the Baptizer."

Salome recoiled. Her eyes widened. Her breath came in labored gasps.

"Do as I tell you," Herodias commanded. "For your sake as well as mine. Should the people take it into their heads to stone me, you will not be spared. The Baptizer must be silenced if we are to live." Triumph gleamed in her eyes.

Terrified at the threat, Salome straightway hurried back to the king. "Give me here on a platter the head of John the Baptizer."

Silence fell over the court. The shock in Herod's eyes showed Salome's demand had partially sobered him. Regret clouded his face, and he opened his mouth, glanced around at the gathered guests, and halted. Salome followed his thoughts. He might be willing to give the other half of his kingdom to undo his rash promise, but he would not. To do so would make him an object of contempt.

Herod gave the command. Soon after, the executioner returned. For a moment Salome stared at the platter. She drove her teeth into her lip to keep down nausea. She closed her ears against the horrid sounds of retching by those sober enough to care. In silence so heavy it hung like a shroud, Salome turned, fixed her gaze straight ahead, and carried her gruesome burden to an ecstatic Herodias.

No one knows if Salome ever wept bitter tears or was haunted by nightmares for her evil deed. History only records that she danced, and John paid with his life for daring to speak out against evil wherever he found it, even in the highest places.

Matthew 14; Mark 6

the canaanite woman, mother of faith

For many years a woman of Canaan cared for her daughter. Grievously vexed with a devil, the girl writhed and threw herself back and forth, wailing and gnashing her teeth until her mother thought she would die. Sometimes her secret heart wished she would. Death could surely be no worse than life as the maiden lived it.

Why had they been so cursed? All who dwelled on the coasts of Tyre and Sidon knew their story and shunned them. How long must a mother watch the one she had given life be destroyed by a devil?

"There is a Jew called Jesus who travels in the land," a neighbor told the distraught woman after the worst spell her daughter had ever suffered. She lowered her voice, as if afraid to be overheard. "It is said He heals those who come to Him."

The mother laughed bitterly. "A Jew heal the daughter of a woman of Canaan? Such a thing could not be!" Yet as the attacks increased, she knew she must pursue every rumor on behalf of her daughter.

When the woman came to Jesus, she immediately began to cry in a loud voice, "Have mercy on me, O Lord, Son of David; my daughter is grievously vexed with a devil," then held her breath waiting for His reply.

Jesus answered not.

She cried again.

The disciples, impatient with her pleadings, besought Jesus, "Send her away, for she cries after us."

But He answered, "I am sent to the lost sheep of the house of Israel."

The woman's hope flickered like a lamp with only a few drops of oil. Should she leave off beseeching Him? Nay. Better to risk the wrath of the One she implored than go away heavy-hearted. She fell at Jesus' feet and worshiped Him, saying, "Lord, help me."

Jesus answered and said, "It is not right to take the children's bread and cast it to dogs."

Goaded by her great need, the woman refused to be silent. She refused to let Jesus walk away, for if He did, all hope must go with Him. "True, Lord. Yet even the dogs eat the crumbs that fall from their masters' table."

She dared not look up, dared not risk looking at Jesus or the disciples who indignantly murmured against her that she should speak so to the Master.

Then Jesus answered her, "O woman, great is your faith; your request is granted." And her daughter was made whole from that very hour.

The woman of Canaan is a permanent reminder of how love and concern for others and faith born of despair can prevail even when circumstances appear hopeless.

Matthew 15; Mark 7

The ten virgins—five wise and five foolish—are characters in a parable Jesus told. A parable is "an earthly story with a heavenly meaning."

"Good friends, our lamps are growing dim," a maiden said to her companions. "We must go forth, buy oil, and fill them, lest they go out before the bridegroom cometh." She reached for her shawl and veil.

Four of the nine virgins she addressed straightway rose up. They went with her into the marketplace and purchased oil to replenish their supply.

"Why do you make haste?" the other five wanted to know. "It is yet day. The bridegroom tarries. There is plenty of time to fill our lamps before he comes." They chattered and laughed together, poking fun at the five virgins industriously filling and polishing their lamps until they shone brightly.

The hour grew late and the household became weary, but no word came from the expected guest. At last, all retired and fell into deep slumber.

At the midnight hour, a great cry sounded throughout the streets of the city. "Behold, the bridegroom cometh; go ye out to meet him."

The ten virgins immediately arose and joyously trimmed their lamps. The five who had failed to fill their lamps cried, "Give us of your oil, for our lamps have gone out."

The others shook their heads. "Not so, lest there be not enough for us and you. But go ye rather to them that sell, and buy for yourselves."

The five foolish virgins who had whiled away their time in mocking their wiser sisters wasted no more time. They rushed into the marketplace, pounded on an oil merchant's door, and clamored for him to open his shop, that they might purchase oil.

The door remained shuttered; the shop dark and bare.

"We must have oil," the frightened girls told one another. "We will try another merchant."

While their companions were out attempting to buy oil, the bridegroom came. Great was the joy of the five virgins who were ready and waiting for him. They went in with him to the marriage feast, and the door was shut behind them.

From dark street to dark street the foolish five ran, beating on doors, trying to rouse anyone who might sell or lend them oil for their empty lamps. They railed against their five wise sisters, saying they should have shared their oil. Yet they knew in their hearts if the situation were reversed, they would not dare give away precious oil and risk not having enough for themselves.

What little oil remained in their lamps had long since vanished. Heavy of heart, the five virgins turned toward home, hoping for some miracle to fill their lamps so that they might be found ready to be admitted to the marriage feast.

At last they reached the house. The door stood firmly shut. All their trying could not open it. "Lord, Lord," they implored. "Open to us."

But he answered and said, "Verily I say unto you, I know you not."

Five foolish virgins huddled together in outer darkness, weeping bitterly at having lost their chance simply because they had not prepared during the time given to make ready.

Historians say a faithfully observed custom in those days was the setting of the marriage time by the bridegroom. He chose any day within a two-week period and made ready, then sent a messenger to announce his arrival. All ten virgins surely knew the custom. Five prepared ahead of time. The other five acted on the premise there was no hurry, with dire results— offering a lesson well worth heeding.

Matthew 25

Never in all his young life had the small boy from Jerusalem been so heartsick or so angry. He lay sleepless on his pallet, fighting hot tears and wishing he could forget the past terrible days. "Judas sold Jesus for thirty pieces of silver," he muttered. "Thirty pieces of silver for One who never did anything but good!"

The boy's rage and despair rose higher. "Pilate could have saved Jesus. He should have released Him instead of Barabbas. Maybe he would have done the right thing if he wasn't so afraid of Caesar." The lad pounded his thin pillow. "Probably not. The miserable coward called for water, washed his hands, and said, 'I am innocent of the blood of this just person,' then told the crowd, 'You see to it.'"

Sharp images rushed through the suffering boy's mind. Although sickened by the horror of the events, he had refused to desert Jesus, as many others had done. There were rumors that even Peter had denied Him.

The boy tossed and turned. Tears streamed onto his pillow as he remembered the procession to Golgotha. When Jesus fell and could no longer bear the weight of the cross, he had tried to get through the crowd to help Him carry the cross. Yet, wiry as he was, he had been unable to reach Jesus. The guards had forced another into service.

"Where were Jesus' disciples?" he brokenly demanded. "Why didn't they step forward?" Only the smothering darkness replied, bringing more scenes so vivid that they felt engraved in his brain. Last and worst was the sight of Jesus hanging on the cross beneath a sign that read: THIS IS JESUS, THE KING OF THE JEWS. Not until He cried out with a loud voice, "It is finished," and bowed His head for the last time, did the watching boy turn away, running as if pursued by a legion of demons.

At last, grief and exhaustion took their toll. He slept. He

awakened to an empty world, a world robbed of Jesus and His love. He ate little, slept less. Instead, he roamed the city streets, listening to those who proclaimed triumph and those who wailed. All the time, something nagged at his brain. Something Jesus had said about rising on the third day after being crucified. Coupled with the rumors that Pilate had placed heavy guards at Jesus' tomb, suspicion arose—and with it a morsel of hope. *What if it is true? What if Jesus will indeed rise on the third day?*

"I will be there and see for myself," the boy resolved. Despite his grandiose plans, his tired body betrayed him. By the time he awakened on the first day of the week, the day was far gone. He sprang up in remorse and stepped outside his home. People danced in the streets. A white-haired man the boy knew to be trustworthy hurried over to him.

"Have you heard the news?" he shouted. "Praise to Jehovah. Jesus has risen from the dead! There was a great earthquake. An angel of heaven came and rolled back the stone from the door of the tomb. The guards became like dead men! The angel told the women who went to prepare His body to go tell His disciples, and Peter, that He goes before them to Galilee. Mary Magdalene has seen and talked with Jesus. He is alive, I tell you!" He grabbed the boy and shook him. "Alive! Come. Let us go to Galilee and see Him for ourselves."

Side by side, the thankful old man and the eager young boy set out for Galilee to find Jesus, on the most wonderful day the world had ever known.

John 19; Matthew 27

pontius pilate, coward

Pontius Pilate was the Roman governor of Palestine in the time of Christ. The last thing he wanted to deal with was some explosively sensitive, incomprehensible altercation among the Jews in Jerusalem. But he was charged with hearing and judging local disputes.

One such dispute raged between the Jewish leaders and Jesus of Nazareth. Jesus was arrested and dragged before Pilate early one morning. Pilate heard the case and questioned Jesus. He was very surprised that Jesus did not respond to the accusations of the chief priests and elders of the Jewish people. He could find nothing that Jesus had done wrong. When Pilate learned that Jesus was a Galilean, he tried to defer judgment to King Herod, who happened to be in Jerusalem at the time. But Herod and his men merely beat and mocked Jesus and sent Him back to Pilate.

Pilate had a diplomatic way out of this mess. He had a custom of releasing a prisoner at the time of the Jewish Passover each year and had in custody a particularly troublesome criminal named Barabbas. "I can give you Barabbas, or I can give you Jesus," Pilate told the people gathered at Jesus' trial. He hoped the crowd would pick Jesus to be released. Then he would not have to deal with the chief priests' claim. But the mob had been stirred up by the Jewish elders. They picked the dreadful Barabbas to be set free.

Pilate's wife had had a very disturbing dream about Jesus. "Have nothing to do with that man," she warned. But Pilate had to do his duty. He asked the mob again whether they wanted him to release Jesus or the criminal Barabbas. "Give us Barabbas!" they demanded. So Pilate washed his hands in front of everyone, meaning that he considered himself free from blame if the innocent man was executed. "Kill Him yourselves," he told the Jewish leaders.

To Pilate, the judgment of Jesus Christ was a harrying annoyance. It may have been a dramatic incident, but at the time he basically regarded his role in one of the most important events in the history of civilization as little more than a distraction from his routine duties.

Matthew 27:1–2, 11–31; Mark 15:1–20; Luke 3:1; 23:1–25; John 18:28–19:22

First, restlessness. Then dreams without form or substance, more terrifying than any the wife of Pontius Pilate, the governor of Judea, had ever known. "No. No!" A scream burst from her throat and tore the fabric of sleep to shreds. She bolted upright and threw back the silken bed coverings that threatened to smother her.

"Mistress, what is it?" Maidens in her service ran to the chamber, eyes enormous in their white faces.

Slowly the hard beating of her heart stilled enough for her to whisper, "Where is my husband?" Perception sharpened by the dream that yet clutched at her with frightening fingers, she caught their hesitation and quick exchange of glances.

"Answer me," she ordered with an imperious gesture.

"Even at this moment he questions a prisoner," one faltered.

"The man called Jesus?"

"Yea."

She sank back against her cushions and waved them away, feeling the blood drain from her face. Jesus, who haunted her dreams until she felt she would go mad. The distraught woman pressed her hands to her aching temples. Why had Pontius Pilate ever consented to accept the post of procurator here in this miserable land? Her lip curled. Enemies in high places were surely responsible for the ignominious assignment. Ever since they arrived, there had been nothing but trouble. In his ignorance of those he had been sent to rule, Pilate had made one mistake after another and incurred the hatred and wrath of his subjects.

"I cannot think of it," the tormented woman cried. Yet how could she not think of it? The entire land of Judea rang with gossip concerning the man who now stood in the judgment hall before her husband.

"Just another rabble-rousing Jew," Pontius had said when he

was told the chief priests and elders had taken counsel against Jesus to put Him to death. Yet in spite of his bold statement, he shifted uneasily. "I don't like this. They bring their squabbles to me when they should be solving them. What good are they if they cannot settle their own disputes?"

"It is more than that," his wife pointed out. "This Jesus has spoken out against the Pharisees and scribes, calling them corrupt, whitewashed sepulchers."

"Perhaps He should be praised rather than condemned." Pilate smiled sardonically. "That bunch of hypocrites is no more qualified to lead than the swine they despise." He sighed. "What must be will be. They have no authority to give an execution order."

"So they come to you," she bitterly told him.

"Yea." He strode out, leaving her to ponder.

Now the wife of Pilate slid from her couch and clapped her hands. When her maidens came running, she ordered them to bring her writing materials and hastily wrote: "Have nothing to do with that just man, for I have suffered many things this day in a dream because of Him."

"See this is taken to the governor at once," she commanded, then paced the floor of her luxurious rooms a long, weary time— until slow, heavy steps announced the coming of her husband. Before he entered, she could tell things had not gone well.

"I washed my hands of it," he mumbled. "I told the multitude I was innocent of the blood of the just man. They said, 'His blood be on us and on our children.'" He stared at his shaking hands, called for a pitcher and water, and washed his hands again.

She said nothing. Pontius continued in a voice so dead it brought shivers to her body. Misery shone in his dull eyes. "I found no fault in Him, but what could I do? They said I was no friend of Caesar if I released Jesus. It is over."

Nay, his wife's heart shouted. *Your misery—and mine—is only beginning.*

Matthew 27

Mary Magdalene, out of whom Jesus had cast seven devils, writhed with pain. The Master had done so much for her. Why could she not have done more for Him? Although she, along with a few other women, had followed Jesus and ministered to Him, all they could do was stand helplessly by and watch Him die on the cross between two thieves.

She and Mary the mother of Joses had sat near the sepulcher, silently grieving. When they went home, the Sabbath passed slowly. How could life continue? Mary thought of herself before Jesus healed her, of the spells that had come over her without warning and turned her into a madwoman. All it had taken to free her was a single touch. She could still feel the warmth that flowed through her, healing her spiritually and cleansing her of all sin.

At last the Sabbath passed. On the first day of the week, at the rising of the sun, Mary Magdalene joined Mary the mother of James and a friend named Salome. Carrying sweet spices to anoint Jesus' body, they came to the sepulcher. "Who shall roll away the stone from the door of the sepulcher, that we may enter?" one asked. The women looked at one another in dismay. After Jesus died and was taken from the cross, Joseph of Arimathaea, an honorable counselor who also waited for the kingdom of God, had boldly gone to Pilate and asked for the body of Jesus. The governor agreed. Joseph brought fine linen and took Jesus down and wrapped Him. He laid Jesus in a sepulcher hewn out of rock. A great stone was rolled over the entrance, and guards were sent by Pilate. Three women, no matter how determined, would not be able to move the stone.

"Behold!" Mary pointed, gasping for breath. "The stone has been rolled away!"

"How. . . ? When. . . ? Where are the guards?"

The entrance to the sepulcher looked wide and empty. The women looked at one another and hesitantly stepped inside. They fell to their knees in fright, for a young man clothed in a long white garment sat on the right side. His countenance was like lightning, and his raiment white as snow.

"Be not affrighted," he said. "Why seek ye the living among the dead? He is not here, but is risen. Remember how He spake unto you when He was yet in Galilee, saying, 'The Son of man must be delivered into the hands of sinful men, and be crucified, and the third day rise again'? But go your way, and tell His disciples and Peter that He goeth before you into Galilee. There shall ye see Him, as He said unto you."

Marveling, unable to believe what they had seen and heard, the women fled. Mary Magdalene went straight to Simon Peter and John. "They have taken away the Lord out of the sepulcher, and we know not where they have laid Him," she cried. In broken phrases, she told the disciples what the angel had said. Peter and John hastened to the sepulcher, but only the linen clothes and napkin lay as mute evidence that one had been there. Unable to understand it, they went to their homes.

Mary could not bear to leave. She stood outside the sepulcher weeping, then bent down and looked in. Two angels in white sat inside, one at the foot, the other at the head of where Jesus' body had lain. They asked why she wept, and she repeated, "Because they have taken away my Lord, and I know not where they have laid Him." Blinded by her tears, she turned and faced a man she supposed to be the gardener.

He said, "Woman, why weepest thou? Whom seekest thou?"

She pleaded for Him to tell her where Jesus had been taken, but He said unto her, "Mary."

That voice! Joy flooded her soul. "Rabboni! Master!"

"Touch Me not, for I am not yet ascended to My Father," Jesus said.

Heart pounding, she ran and found the disciples. They believed not, for they had not seen. But Mary of Magdala knew

Jesus lived again, even as she lived anew when Jesus cast out the seven devils and made her a new creature in Him.

Matthew 27; Mark 15–16; John 20

barabbas, prisoner set free

"Give us Barabbas!"

The prisoner cringed as he heard the mob outside the Roman governor's house. Had his time come so soon? The famous criminal Barabbas was awaiting execution. His crimes: murder, theft, and insurrection. Dragged before the Roman governor Pilate, Barabbas was outwardly defiant but inwardly terrified. The crowd was screaming for blood—his blood. But wait. Barabbas listened again to the shouting crowd. They did not want his blood; they were demanding his freedom!

Another prisoner was present, bound, beaten, and bleeding. He was Jesus the Nazarene who claimed to be the Messiah. Barabbas had heard of this man and His many miracles. Jesus, they said, healed the sick, confounded the wisdom of the scribes and Pharisees, and even raised the dead to life. Yet there He was, tortured and humiliated. Pilate gestured to Jesus and then to Barabbas and asked the bloodthirsty crowd, "Which of these men do you want me to set free?"

Everyone knew that during the yearly Passover celebration, Pilate's custom was to release a prisoner of the people's choosing. On this occasion their choice was between the untainted and the terrorist—Jesus and Barabbas. Barabbas could not believe his ears. Not only had the surging crowd chosen him to live, but he would be set free!

Then Pilate washed his hands as a symbol that he was not responsible for taking Jesus' innocent life. It was the crowd (or the crowd's instigators) who were to bear this liability. He ordered Barabbas released and Jesus scourged.

Barabbas said nothing as he waited impatiently for the guards to unshackle him and did not pause to watch the flogging of the Nazarene. Fearful that the people would change their minds, Barabbas fled into the morning, retreated to the back streets of Jerusalem, and disappeared from history.

One may ask, did Barabbas ever wonder about the innocent man who had taken his cross that day—the one who died in his place? Did he repent? Did he believe? Or did the reprieved Barabbas continue to live as a criminal? Does he live today in the understanding of New Testament readers as the model of all of humanity—deserving of death but released to life by the sacrifice of God's Son?

Matthew 27:15–26; Mark 15:6–15; Luke 23:13–25; John 18:39–40

mark, early church leader

The young disciple Mark was eager to spread the wonderful news of Jesus Christ, especially to the non-Jewish world. His Gospel is the shortest of the four, and possibly was the first to be written.

Mark's enthusiasm shows in his action-oriented writing. He skips altogether the story of the Savior's birth and begins his account with Jesus' baptism by John the Baptist at the onset of His ministry. By the end of the first chapter of the Gospel of Mark, Jesus has already resisted Satan, chosen four disciples, and performed many miracles of healing and exorcism.

Mark labored with Paul, Peter, Barnabas, and others to build up the early church. It is thought that Mark was martyred like his fellow workers. According to one account, Mark was dragged to death through the streets of Alexandria.

Mark; Acts 12:12, 25; 13:5, 13; 15:36–39; Colossians 4:10–11; 2 Timothy 4:11; Philemon 23–24; 1 Peter 5:13

A small girl and her mother stood a little apart from a group of men gathered near a village well. "I tell you, it's true," a gray-bearded man insisted, waving his hands wildly in the still air. "It happened in Capernaum. Within the hour, word of it ran through the village like a dog after a quail!"

"What happened? What are you talking about?" a younger man demanded.

"Jesus, son of Joseph, the carpenter, has set loose tongues wagging again."

"It isn't the first time and won't be the last," someone sneered. An unpleasant laugh followed.

The little girl buried her fingers in her mother's tunic. "Why do they speak so of Jesus?" she whispered. "I thought He did good things."

"Hush, child. He does, but if the men see that we are listening to them, they will send us away," her mother warned. "I want to hear more about Jesus."

So do I, the little girl thought but wisely kept the words locked behind her lips.

"Well?" a dark-eyed man challenged. "What has this Jesus done now?"

"Plenty." The man with the news paused. "He must be a diviner, for when He and His disciples came to Capernaum, He asked why they had been disputing along the way. No one would answer, but Jesus knew. I don't know how, but He did. He told the Twelve, 'If anyone desires to be first, he shall be last of all and servant of all.' "

The listening child's mouth formed a little round O. Her mother was a servant in a wealthy man's home, but never first in anything.

The speaker ignored the indignant murmur that began.

His eyes glistened. "That isn't all. Jesus took a little child and set him in the midst of the disciples. He took the child in His arms and said whoever caused a little one who believed in Him to stumble, it would be better for him if a millstone were hung around his neck and he were thrown into the sea!"

"With that kind of talk, soon our children will be rising up against us," someone objected. "Has He forgotten that children are to honor their fathers and mothers? Or does He throw away the Law of Moses?"

"Come, daughter," the woman whispered. "We must go."

"Mother, will you take me to see Jesus?" the child pleaded, trotting beside her mother.

"Yes, if He comes near to where we are."

"I am glad." The little girl skipped along. "I hope He will come soon."

Before long, her wish came true. Jesus came to the region of Judea by the other side of the Jordan. As usual, a great multitude of people gathered to hear His teachings. Among them were the woman and her daughter. Unfortunately, the crowd was so great they could not get near Him.

"Please, let us through," the mother pleaded. "I want Jesus to touch my child and bless her."

"Woman, be gone," some of the disciples said. "Jesus is too busy for children."

Jesus heard them and was greatly displeased. "Let the little children come to Me, and forbid them not, for of such is the kingdom of God. . . . Whoever does not receive the kingdom of God as a little child will by no means enter it."

One by one, Jesus took the children up in His arms and blessed them. When it was the little girl's turn, she looked deep into the kind eyes that smiled at her. Long after she forgot the words of Jesus' blessing, she remembered the look in the Master's eyes.

Mark 9–10; Luke 18

Everywhere Jesus went, people followed, eager to see any new attraction that would interrupt the monotony of their daily lives. They had one thing in common: a desire to witness for themselves the things they had heard were happening in the villages and cities and along the dusty highways that Jesus visited.

A lad who had lost his parents and had no kinfolk to care for him decided to go see Jesus. Long accustomed to looking after himself, he secreted food inside his tunic and set out on his quest. Who knew what might happen? If Jesus was as good and kind as people said He was, perhaps He had room in His band of followers for an enterprising young boy to carry messages or serve in other ways.

After several days, he saw a band of travelers in the distance. He hurried toward them. "Is Jesus here?" he demanded, pulse racing.

"Over there. He speaks with one who came to Him," a turbaned man said.

The boy worked his way through the disciples until he stood behind a man kneeling before a robed figure. "Good Master," the man said. "What shall I do that I may inherit eternal life?"

The boy eagerly looked at Jesus and then rejoiced. He looked good and kind, just as people said.

"Why do you call Me good?" Jesus asked. "No one is good but One, that is, God. You know the commandments: 'Do not commit adultery,' 'Do not murder,' 'Do not steal,' 'Do not bear false witness,' 'Do not defraud,' 'Honor your father and your mother.' "

"Master, all these I have observed from my youth."

The lad smiled. He, too, had kept these sayings, even though when he grew hungry and there was little work, he had been tempted to steal food. Now he stared into the Master's face.

Jesus said, "One thing you lack: Go your way, sell whatever you have, and give to the poor, and you will have treasure in heaven. And come, take up the cross, and follow Me."

A murmur rose. "The man has great possessions," someone whispered.

The kneeling figure stood and walked away. The boy thought he had never seen a sadder face.

Jesus looked around at His disciples. "How hard it is for those who trust in riches to enter the kingdom of God!"

For the first time, the boy was glad he had no riches that might keep him out of the kingdom of God. Even so, he dared not approach Jesus and ask if he might become a follower. Instead, he tagged along behind the others, unwilling to leave Jesus.

In Jericho, he was able to get a bit of work and replenish his store of food, but when Jesus and His disciples left the city, he followed. So did a great crowd of people. Soon they came upon a blind man sitting beside the road begging.

"Jesus, Son of David, have mercy on me!" Bartimaeus cried.

"Be quiet!" unfriendly voices warned, but the blind man only cried louder. When Jesus commanded him to be called, Bartimaeus threw aside his garment, rose, and came forth.

"What do you want Me to do for you?" Jesus asked.

"Lord, I want to receive my sight."

During this exchange, the boy who followed Jesus had wriggled through the crowd. At the beggar's bold request, he felt excitement flow through his veins. Would Jesus heal anyone as unimportant as Bartimaeus?

"Go your way; your faith has made you whole," Jesus said.

Immediately the beggar's blind eyes were opened. He shouted for joy and followed Jesus on the road, along with the boy who had witnessed a miracle.

Mark 10

A small boy who lived in Jerusalem loved to perch high on his grandfather's broad shoulders as he strode the city streets. From his vantage point, the child could observe everything that was going on and report to his grandfather.

Late one afternoon, his grandfather rushed into their humble home. "I am sorry you weren't with me today," he said. "Never have I beheld a sight such as what just unfolded before my eyes."

"Don't be sad, Grandfather," the boy comforted. "While you were gone I prepared our meal." He waved toward the cheese, grapes, and loaf of bread he had set out. "What did you see?"

The old man dropped to a mat, blessed the food, and answered, "I saw a man riding on a colt."

Childish laughter rang out. "Why, Grandfather! We have seen many men riding on many colts."

"Not like this man," his grandfather said. "His name is Jesus. His followers had spread their garments on the colt. Many spread garments on the road before Him. Others cut down leafy branches from nearby trees and covered the road. They cried, 'Hosanna! Blessed is He who comes in the name of the Lord!' "

Excitement restored youth to his face. "Child, do you know what this means?"

The boy wrinkled his forehead. "I—"

"It is a fulfillment of what was written by the prophets of old. Zechariah prophesied the Promised One would come riding on a colt." He wiped moisture from his eyes. "Surely this Jesus must be the Messiah for whom we have waited so long!"

The boy trembled with excitement. Jewish children were taught about the Messiah from the time they were in their cradles. "Oh, Grandfather, I wish I had been there!" he exclaimed. The piece of bread he had taken fell from his fingers.

"Eat, child. Tomorrow we will go to the temple. Perhaps we shall see Jesus."

Sleep did not come easily for either the boy or his grandfather. Early the next day, they rose, ate a simple meal, and started for the temple. As usual, the boy rode on his grandfather's shoulders. The old man never seemed to tire of carrying him.

"Grandfather, there are doves flying out of the temple," the small boy shouted. "Look, the money changers are running after them!"

His grandfather elbowed his way through the crowd, just as another man fled from the temple. His face was black with anger, his voice harsh with fright. "The man has gone mad," he screamed. "Jesus has turned over our tables. He is driving out all who buy and sell in the temple!" A hint of froth whitened his beard. "He will not allow anyone to carry wares through the temple."

As the boy and his grandfather approached the temple grounds, they heard a stern voice.

"Is it not written, 'My house shall be called a house of prayer for all nations'? But you have made it a 'den of thieves.' "

The next moment the boy caught sight of a robed man striding from the temple. "I see Jesus," he shrilled. "Oh, Grandfather, He is gone! You did not get to see Him!"

"Ah, but I saw Him yesterday," his grandfather said. "I am glad you saw Jesus. Promise me that you will always remember this day."

"I promise," the child said.

He kept his promise. Even though he grew to be older than his grandfather, the small boy never forgot seeing Jesus the day He cleansed the temple.

Mark 11

Jesus loved to watch people. He yearned over them and longed for them to break the bondage formed by sin and be free. He rejoiced when they listened to Him and laid aside their burdens, prejudices, and hypocrisy. He wept when they turned away—but always, He watched.

One day He sat watching those who came to the treasury and cast in their money. He noticed the careless way the rich flung in much, then went away with heads held high, proud to have done their duty so magnificently. Perhaps He sadly smiled, knowing they had their reward by being seen and noted for their generosity.

A poor widow hung back until the more worthy finished making their offerings, then she timidly came forward. Evidence of poverty showed in her clothing and in the work-worn hands that had obviously known great toil. Her tired fingers fumbled in her cloak and drew forth two mites, which make a farthing.

For a moment, she stared at the small amount of money, then cast it in with the rest. She disappeared into the crowd, little dreaming her deed would be known until time ran out.

Jesus called unto Him His disciples. He said to them, "Verily I say unto you that this poor widow hath cast more in than all they which have cast into the treasury."

The disciples looked at one another in amazement. How could the two mites, which make a farthing, compare with the golden coins thrown into the treasury by those of great wealth?

Jesus went on to explain. "All they did cast in of their abundance; but she of her want did cast in all that she had, even all her living."

As the widow of Zerephath gave the last of her meal and oil to the prophet Elijah, so the woman in Jesus' time gave everything she had. If she could speak to us down the path from the past, perhaps this devoted servant would tell of blessings as great as those experienced by her giving counterpart who lived hundreds of years earlier.

Mark 12; Luke 12

luke, physician

Which of the four authors of the Gospels was a medical doctor? Whose meticulous, methodical writing style gives him away? It was Luke.

This thorough biblical writer handed down parables and details about Jesus' life that are found nowhere else. For example, Luke sought to convince readers that Jesus Christ came back to life physically after the crucifixion. To accomplish this, the writer pointed out that the resurrected Savior ate fish with His disciples. This unique bit of evidence emphasizes a physical resurrection.

Luke also wrote the book of Acts as a continuation of his gospel. It chronicles the spread of Christ's church during the first century. Luke accompanied the apostle Paul through Asia and Macedonia. This book of New Testament history shows how the early Christians struggled not only to spread the gospel, but to understand how the gospel applied to their world.

Tradition says that Luke met a martyr's death, hanged on an olive tree in Greece.

Luke; Acts

elisabeth and zacharias, parents of john the baptist

Mary's cousin Elisabeth lived with her husband, Zacharias, in the hill country of Judah. Word of their righteousness spread throughout the land, for they walked blamelessly in all the commandments and ordinances of the Lord. Yet one thing they lacked: a child. Elisabeth was barren, and both she and Zacharias were aged.

Zacharias served in the priest's office and burned incense in the temple of the Lord. One day an angel appeared and stood on the right side of the altar. Fear fell on the old priest. But the angel said, "Fear not. Thy prayer is heard, and thy wife, Elisabeth, shall bear thee a son, and thou shalt call his name John."

The angel said John would be great in the Lord's sight, many would rejoice at his birth, and he would be filled with the Holy Ghost even from his mother's womb. But Zacharias could not believe. "Whereby shall I know this? For I am an old man, and my wife well stricken in years."

The angel announced that he was Gabriel, sent by God. Because of Zacharias's unbelief, he would be dumb—unable to speak—until all had been accomplished.

Elisabeth conceived. Great was the old couple's joy, but the priest remained mute. Elisabeth sang at her work and dreamed of the day she would deliver her firstborn. How good God was to remove her barren state and thereby take away her reproach among men!

In the sixth month, Mary came to pay Elisabeth a visit. The moment Mary saluted her cousin, Elisabeth felt her babe leap within her. She blessed Mary and the babe she carried within her. Mary responded with a song of praise.

For three happy months, Mary dwelled with Elisabeth. How they talked, the two who had been chosen to be mothers in Israel: one of the Son of God, the other of one who would turn many hearts toward the Lord. After Mary returned to her home, Elisabeth brought forth a son. Her heart swelled with pride when her neighbors and her cousins heard how the Lord had showed great mercy. They rejoiced with her—but Zacharias remained mute.

Elisabeth wondered if he would ever speak again. She contented herself in caring for her son, little heeding those who protested when she said he should be called John.

"There is none of thy kindred called by this name," they protested, when on the eighth day the child was brought for circumcision.

They made signs to Zacharias. He called for writing materials and confirmed the baby should be called John. Immediately his tongue was loosed. He praised God and prophesied of that to come.

Elisabeth cherished her son, yet she never forgot the prophecies concerning him. Scripture does not tell whether she lived to see John grow and wax strong in spirit. Did she watch him enter the desert, where he would abide until his time came? Was she one who entered the waters of baptism at his hand? If alive at the time, surely she agonized when an act of wanton wickedness ended his ministry. All that is known is the exemplary life of this godly mother of John the Baptizer who fulfilled her role and rejoiced at having been blessed in her old age.

Luke 1

anna and simeon meet Jesus

Following the birth of Jesus, Mary and Joseph left Bethlehem. They traveled to Jerusalem so Jesus could be blessed in the temple when he was eight days old, as was the custom.

At the time Jesus was born, a certain man named Simeon lived in Jerusalem. He had loved and served God all the days of his life, and he was filled with the Holy Spirit. Simeon eagerly awaited the coming of the Promised One, whom the prophets of old had foretold would someday come to deliver God's people from bondage. If only he, God's humble servant, could live to see that day, he would die in peace.

God was pleased with Simeon. He knew the desires of the devout man's heart. God promised Simeon he would not die until he had seen the Son of God.

Many years passed. Simeon's heart leaped within him when Mary and Joseph brought Jesus to the temple. He realized that the promise God had made to him had come to pass. Simeon joyfully took Jesus up into his arms. He blessed God, crying, "Lord, now let Your servant depart in peace, according to Your word. I have seen Your salvation, which You prepared before the face of all people, a light to bring revelation to the Gentiles and the glory of Your people Israel."

Mary and Joseph marveled when Simeon spoke of their tiny son. Then Simeon turned to them. He blessed them and said to Mary, "This child is destined for the fall and rising of many in Israel, and to be a sign that will be spoken against. Yea, a sword shall pierce through your own soul also, that the thoughts of many hearts may be revealed."

At that very instant, they were interrupted by someone else in the temple that day. Anna was eighty-four years old. Her husband had died many years before, after he and Anna had only been married seven years. Anna served God in the temple, fasting and praying both day and night. She was a prophetess, one whom God had chosen to discern many things that would happen before they took place.

When Mary and Joseph brought Jesus to the temple, Anna's heart pounded in her aged chest like someone knocking on a door, demanding entrance. Just as Simeon had realized the truth minutes earlier, so Anna also knew through the Holy Spirit that Jesus was God's gift to the world. She knew that God had sent Him so everyone who listened to His words and believed on Him could be saved from their sins and one day live in heaven with God and Jesus. She gave thanks to the Lord and spoke to Him of all those who looked for redemption in Jerusalem.

Jesus was just a baby. He was too young to know all these things. Too young to know that for many, many years holy men of God had told of His coming. Too young to know that the prophet Isaiah had long ago said He would be called Wonderful, Counselor, the mighty God, the everlasting Father, the

Prince of Peace. Yet all those things, and much more, happened after Jesus was blessed in the temple.

For now, Joseph and Mary pondered what Simeon and Anna had said. Then, having fulfilled the requirements of the Law of Moses, they traveled back to their own city, Nazareth in Galilee.

Luke 2

Jesus is missing!

During the next few years, Jesus grew to be strong and wise. Every year His parents went to Jerusalem for what was called the Feast of the Passover. This observance reminded Jews how God had taken care of them long ago when they were in the land of Egypt.

What a time of joy and excitement! Families traveled caravan style, camping together along the way and making the most of the pilgrimage that became a holiday, especially for the younger members in the noisy group.

The year Jesus was twelve, He also went to Jerusalem for the holiday. Surely His boyish heart beat faster at the thought of being with the family and friends who thronged the roads on their way to Jerusalem! In the way of young boys ever since time began, the opportunity to see a world far different from His own must have heightened His senses to all that surrounded Him: dusty roads; the clamor of the multitude and the bray of donkeys; the sight and sound of Roman soldiers on patrol, ordering the people to make way; the pungent odor of sweat and camel dung that assaulted His nostrils; the welcome taste of water from a goatskin bag.

When they reached their destination and looked into the city, Jerusalem in all its glory lay before them. Jerusalem, a city of unexplored wonders for those visiting it for the first time since being brought as tiny babies by their parents to be blessed. How different from Nazareth! The most awe-inspiring sight was the temple, the place that all devout Jews believed to be the dwelling place on earth of the one High God.

Those who came to Jerusalem always stayed for several days before turning their steps back to their homeland. They would cherish the memories of the Feast of the Passover until another year passed and the time to return to offer sacrifices and pay homage to their God came again.

After the holiday ended, the large group began the journey home. On the second day, Mary went to Joseph. She looked worried. "Do you know where Jesus is?" she asked.

"Perhaps He is among our kinfolk and acquaintances," Joseph said.

"I cannot find Him," Mary told him.

From family to family they went, searching for the missing boy. He was nowhere to be found. Jesus must have been left behind in Jerusalem! His parents looked at one another in alarm. How would a twelve-year-old boy get along in the great city?

Mary and Joseph left the others and hurried back to Jerusalem. After three frightening days of looking for Jesus, they found Him in the temple. He was listening and talking with the wise men there. All those who heard were surprised that such a young boy could know so much.

When Mary and Joseph saw and heard Him, they were amazed. Could this be Jesus, their son, debating with those so much older and wiser than He?

After a moment, Mary said, "Son, why have You done this to us? Your father and I have been searching for You with great sorrow."

Jesus told her, "Why did You seek Me? Didn't you know that I must be about My Father's business?"

Mary and Joseph did not understand what He meant by saying such a thing.

Jesus went back to Nazareth with them and obeyed everything they told Him to do. He continued to grow and learn. Mary kept all these sayings in her heart.

Many years passed. One day Jesus knew it was time for Him to leave His home. He needed to go tell all who would listen how much God, their Father, loved them.

Luke 2

a woman of the city

A woman of the city known to be a sinner learned that Jesus of Nazareth had consented to eat with Simon, a Pharisee. She considered and planned what she would do. The Master deserved tribute; she had the means to give it to Him.

While they sat for their meal, she entered Simon's house, carrying in both hands her most precious possession: an alabaster box of ointment. She stood at Jesus' feet and wept, then washed His feet with her tears. She used her long and lustrous hair to dry them, then kissed the Master's feet and anointed them with ointment.

Simon glared at her. She could read his displeasure in the gaze he turned toward her. To have such as she dare to enter his home and minister to Jesus was beyond decency. If He were the prophet people proclaimed, surely He would know her for a sinner and refuse to allow her to touch Him.

Jesus suddenly spoke, addressing his host. "There was a certain creditor who had two debtors: The one owed five hundred pence, and the other fifty. And when they had nothing to pay, he frankly forgave them both. Tell Me, therefore, which of them will love him most?"

Simon answered, "I suppose he who was forgiven most."

Jesus smiled. "You have rightly judged." He turned to the woman but said unto Simon, "See this woman? I entered your house, and you gave Me no water for my feet. But she has washed My feet with her tears and wiped them with her hair.

"You gave Me no kiss, but this woman since the time I came in has not ceased to kiss My feet. My head with oil you did not anoint, but this woman has anointed My feet with ointment.

"Therefore I say to you, her sins, which are many, are forgiven; for she loved much. But to whom little is forgiven, the same loves little."

Jesus said unto her, "Your sins are forgiven."

The woman kneeling at his feet could speak no word. Never since she became notorious had a man spoken to her so. She felt as though she had stepped under a fall of clear water, cleansing and pure.

A quick glance around the circle of watching guests showed their confusion, their inner wonderings of who Jesus could be to forgive sins.

Jesus told her, "Your faith has saved you; go in peace."

Somehow she managed to rise and sedately leave the room, although she longed to leap into the air and cry out with joy. Somehow she made her way down a street that looked far different from when she had trod it on the way to Simon's abode. Jesus' admonition rang in her ears. "Go in peace." Peace! Something she had dreamed about and never thought to find. Now, in a twinkling, it had come.

The alabaster box was empty, but the woman's heart filled to bursting. A new life beckoned. She raised her face to the sky and ran to greet her vastly changed future.

Luke 7

mary and martha, sisters of different priorities

Mary and her sister, Martha's, reputation for hospitality was known throughout their village. They delighted in opening their home to passersby in need of food and lodging. The women invited Jesus to stay with them anytime He came to Bethany.

Mary delighted in sitting at Jesus' feet and hearing His teaching—even when Martha needed help preparing and serving food and with the many tasks necessary to keep a household in good order.

Martha loved to have Jesus stay with them, but it meant much extra work. At times she felt overwhelmed by the magnitude of the task she faced. Sometimes Jesus' disciples accompanied Him. Always curious neighbors dropped by. She could not send them home at mealtimes for fear of being considered ill-mannered, so they, too, must be fed.

On one such occasion, Martha's resentment rose to a full boil. More than the usual number of guests had appeared, and where was Mary when most needed? Where else? Sitting at the Master's feet, listening to His words.

A pang went through Martha, and a lump formed in her throat. If only she could also sit at the Master's feet and hear what He said. Why didn't Mary realize the burden she placed on her sister? Why didn't she offer to take her place supervising the endless chores, the roasting and baking, the bread making and serving? A little voice inside reminded her she wasn't being fair. Mary did her share of cooking and cleaning. She just couldn't bear to be out of Jesus' sight when He came, even to help with the serving.

"Suppose I just walked away from my tasks and joined her?" Martha muttered. "Fine thing. None would be given food or drink until their bellies loudly protested."

Cumbered with much serving, Martha came to Jesus. "Lord, dost Thou not care that my sister hath left me to serve alone? Bid her therefore that she help me."

Mary rose, a stricken look on her face. It was always thus. She became so engrossed in the Master's words as He spoke with her brother, Lazarus, and others who gathered, she forgot her duties. Like a child, she stood with bowed head and quivering lips. What must Jesus think of her? She scarcely dared raise her head enough to look at either Him or Martha.

Jesus hesitated a long moment. He sighed and spoke in

a voice that held more sadness than condemnation. "Martha, Martha," He said. "Thou art careful and troubled about many things."

Mary saw the pleased look creep over her sister's face. Such was high praise from the Master. But why did He address Martha instead of her slothful sister?

Mary held her breath as Jesus continued.

"One thing is needful, and Mary hath chosen that good part, which shall not be taken away from her."

The constricting bands about Mary's heart loosened at His words. She caught quick tears in Martha's eyes, the look of shame at having complained. Martha looked cut to the quick.

Tenderhearted Mary sprang to her sister's side. She wrapped her arms around Martha. "I will help you," she promised. "Then we both shall sit at Jesus' feet."

Readers of the Mary and Martha story often dwell on Jesus' rebuke to Martha and praise of Mary. Yet Jesus did not consider Martha a bad person. On the other hand, He freely praised her for being "careful and troubled about many things." When He pointed out one thing was needed in her life, it didn't mean for her to give up doing the daily chores that require attention. Jesus well knew the necessity of hard labor from lessons learned at Joseph's knee in the carpenter shop and from watching His mother perform household duties.

In saying Mary had chosen that good part that would not be taken from her, Jesus wanted Martha to focus on what was even more important. He would not always abide in the home at Bethany. Martha must learn to store up His teachings, as Mary did, against the time of His departure. Everyday duties would always abound. The opportunity for the sisters to hear Him would not.

Luke 10; John 11–12

Lazarus lay ill, little caring or responding to his sisters' tender ministrations. In spite of everything they could do, he grew worse. Martha and Mary called a servant and ordered, "Go to Jesus and say unto Him, 'Lord, behold, he whom Thou lovest is sick.'" They watched the servant hasten to obey, a measure of comfort stealing into their hearts. In a short time, Jesus would come and all would be well.

Minutes dragged into anxious hours, but Jesus did not come. "Did you not make clear how sick Lazarus is?" Martha demanded of the servant.

"Yea, mistress."

"Then why does He not come?" she cried. "It has been two days."

Lower and lower Lazarus sank until no life remained in him. Martha and Mary could not understand why Jesus tarried along the way. They sadly prepared their brother for burial, hot tears falling on the linen wrappings. They laid him to rest in a cave and rolled a stone before it. The entire household went into mourning for the brother and master who would be with them no more.

"Jesus could have saved Lazarus," Martha bitterly told Mary.

"I know." Her sister sighed, her eyes filled with trouble.

Many of the Jews came to comfort the bereaved women. Days later, word came that Jesus was approaching Bethany. Martha laid aside her tasks and hurried to meet Him, but Mary sat still in the house. When Martha reached Jesus, she burst into tears. "Lord, if Thou hadst been here, my brother had not died. But I know, that even now, whatsoever Thou wilt ask of God, God will give it Thee."

Jesus said unto her, "Thy brother shall rise again."

"I know." Martha sobbed, desolate at the loss of the brother she loved and had cared for so long. "He shall rise again in the resurrection at the last day."

"I am the resurrection and the life; he that believeth in Me, though he were dead, yet shall he live. And whosoever liveth and believeth in Me shall never die. Believest thou this?"

All Jesus' teachings rushed back to confirm the truth to the sorrowful woman. She cried in a voice that held not only faith, but knowledge: "Yea, Lord: I believe that Thou art the Christ, the Son of God, which should come into the world." Then she went back to the house and whispered to Mary, "The Master is come, and calleth for thee."

Jesus had not yet entered the town. When the Jews saw Mary rise up and go to meet Him, they murmured, "She goeth unto the grave to weep," and followed her, as did Martha.

Mary reached Jesus and fell at His feet. "Lord, if Thou hadst been here, my brother had not died."

Jesus groaned in His spirit and was troubled. "Where have ye laid him?"

The Jews said, "Lord, come and see."

Jesus wept, and the Jews murmured among themselves, "Behold how He loved him!" But some said, "Could not this man, which opened the eyes of the blind, have caused that even this man should not have died?"

Martha's broken heart echoed the question over and over as she stumbled after Jesus on the way to the grave.

"Take ye away the stone," Jesus commanded.

"Lord, by this time he stinketh, for he hath been dead four days."

Jesus told her, "Said I not unto thee that if thou wouldst believe, thou shouldest see the glory of God?" Martha didn't understand and shrank back when the stone, with much grinding, moved away from the grave.

Jesus prayed to His Father in heaven, then cried in a loud voice, "Lazarus, come forth." Martha gasped and huddled close to Mary. The watching Jews stood as if frozen. A white figure appeared, bound hand and foot with grave clothes and face covered with a napkin. "Loose him and let him go," Jesus ordered. In fear and trembling, it was done. Lazarus stood before them, strong, whole, resurrected from the dead.

With one accord, those present fell to the ground. They rubbed their eyes, unable to believe what they saw. Many of the Jews who had come to comfort Mary and Martha and seen the things Jesus did, believed on Him from that day.

It is interesting to note that Martha, once gently reproved by the Master, showed such strong faith that she cried affirmation from the midst of tragedy. Out of a broken heart came her unshakable belief in the resurrection.

Martha should be remembered for her valiant testimony that Jesus was the Son of God.

Luke 10; John 11–12

zacchaeus, man with a changed heart

This little man had a big job: He was chief tax collector in Jericho. This made him both rich and despised, because he collected taxes from the common people to give to Rome. Yet even he was interested in the famous teacher and healer from Nazareth.

Jesus was coming into the city. Zacchaeus struggled to catch a glimpse of Him through the throng of people. But he was too short to see anything. So he ran ahead of the procession and climbed up a sycamore tree beside the road. From here he could see everyone—and everyone could see him.

Jesus stopped beneath the tree. "Come down, Zacchaeus," the Master called. "I'm coming to stay at your house today."

The crowd thought it strange that Jesus would associate with someone they considered a sinner. But while Jesus was at his house, Zacchaeus changed their minds. He announced he would give half his possessions to the poor and return four times the amount of money he had collected dishonestly.

"Salvation has come to this house today," Jesus said and reminded His critics, "I came to seek and to save those who are lost."

Luke 19:1–10

the woman at the well

The Samaritan woman turned slow steps toward Jacob's well. She hated going there. Her neighbors pulled their skirts aside when she passed by and murmured against her. Yet she must have water if she was to live, and the sixth hour was as good a time to draw water as any.

Raising her head, she noted a man sitting nearby. He looked tired. His garments showed him to be a Jew. Dread filled her. It was bad enough being the object of scorn among her own kind, but the smug, self-righteous Jews who came to the well as they passed through Samaria made her feel less than the dirt beneath their sandals. She silently stepped forward to draw water so she could leave at once. A pleasant voice halted her, saying, "Give Me to drink."

She looked full in His face, and her lips curled. "How is it that Thou, being a Jew, askest drink of me, which am a woman of Samaria? For the Jews have no dealings with the Samaritans." If the stranger had the brains of a donkey, He would know this and not have to be told.

"If thou knewest the gift of God, and who it is that saith to thee, 'Give Me to drink,' thou wouldest have asked of Him, and He would have given thee living water," He told her.

Living water? Amazed at His manner of speaking, she retorted, "Sir, Thou hast nothing to draw with, and the well is deep: from whence then hast Thou that living water? Art Thou greater than our father Jacob, which gave us the well, and drank thereof himself, and his children, and his cattle?"

Jesus told her whoever drank water from Jacob's well thirsted again, but those who drank of the water He gave would never thirst. He said, "The water that I give him shall be in him a well of water springing up into everlasting life."

Why should the strange words churn her spirit? Suppose this magician could give her water so she never again had to thirst or come to the well and draw? She impulsively pleaded with Him to do so, but Jesus bade her to go, call her husband, and come back to the well.

Shame reddened her face, and she cast her gaze downward to escape His piercing look. "I have no husband." To her amazement, He responded she had spoken well, for although she had had five husbands, the man she now had was not her husband.

Fear came upon her. "Sir, I perceive that Thou art a prophet."

He expounded many things to her. With each truth, her spirit kindled until it flamed into response. "I know that Messiah cometh, which is called Christ. When He is come, He will tell us all things."

Jesus said, "I that speak unto thee am He."

The woman straightway left her water jar. She raced to the city and said unto the people, "Come, see a man which told me all things that ever I did. Is not this the Christ?" She ran to others, proclaiming what had come to pass that day to all who would listen. They went out of the city and came to Him. Many believed on Him by reason of the woman's testimony. They besought Him to tarry, and Jesus abode there two days.

Many more believed because of Jesus' own word, for they had heard Him themselves and knew He was indeed the Christ, the Savior of the world. The Samaritan woman found a niche in history because she listened, believed, and shouted the truth of Jesus, the Christ, through the streets of her city.

***

John 4

From village to village, city to city, Jesus traveled. News of His coming never failed to create a stir among the people.

As the time of the Jewish Passover drew near, word reached those by the Sea of Galilee, also called the Sea of Tiberias, that Jesus was on His way.

"Jesus is going to speak on the mountainside," people shouted. "Come. Let us hurry to see Him. Perhaps He will heal someone, as He has done in other places."

A huge crowd soon assembled and followed Jesus and His disciples. A certain young lad, who was determined not to be left behind, trotted after them. Unlike others who foolishly took no food with them, the boy gathered up five small barley loaves and two small fish. Growling stomachs made it hard to listen, even to someone who was said to be a great Teacher!

As the multitude streamed after Jesus, the boy listened hard to hear what they were saying.

"Jesus heals sick people."

"He makes blind eyes see. He opens deaf ears so people can hear."

"Jesus makes lame people walk."

The lad's mouth dropped open in amazement. Did Jesus really, truly do all those wonderful things? Would He heal someone today?

It took time to climb up the side of the mountain. The lad was glad for the abundant grass beneath his bare feet. It tickled his toes. The only problem was, he couldn't see Jesus very well because of all the tall people around him.

Inch by inch, he squirmed his way through the crowd until he reached the front row. There he planted his tired feet on the ground, crossed his arms, and waited for Jesus to make a miracle.

Instead, Jesus said, "Where can we buy bread for these people to eat?"

The boy looked around him. He could hear the sound of more and more people coming up behind him. He grinned. Jesus didn't have to worry about feeding *him*. He had his lunch right there ready to be eaten whenever he got hungry.

Philip, one of the disciples, looked worried. He told Jesus it would cost a great deal of money for everyone there to have even a bite of food.

Just then Peter's brother Andrew looked straight at the lad who had brought a lunch. "This boy has five small barley loaves and two little fish," he told Jesus. "But what are they among so many?"

The little boy stared. He was awfully hungry. Did Jesus want him to give away his loaves and fishes? Andrew was right. What good would they do? Thousands of people had gathered on the hillside. The boy's stomach growled, but he held out his small supply of food. At least Jesus would have something to eat.

Jesus thanked God for the food. Then something strange happened. Something wonderful. Jesus began handing bread and fish to His disciples. They gave it to the people—five thousand men, as well as women and children. The food kept coming until everyone had all they could eat, even the small boy. And there were twelve baskets of food left over!

The little boy rubbed his eyes. "I don't understand it," he whispered. "How could He make so much out of five small loaves and two fish? I do know one thing. There isn't anyone here today who will ever forget what Jesus did with my lunch!"

John 6

the woman accused

The wretched woman brought to the temple by the scribes and Pharisees dared not raise her head, yet in spite of her terror, she felt a certain sense of release. Today would end her miserable life. If it weren't for the agony to come with the sharp stones hurled by men no better than she, she wouldn't care. Perhaps the gods would be merciful and allow the first to stun or fell her with a blow to the head.

"Master, this woman was taken in adultery, in the very act. Now Moses in the law commanded us that such should be stoned. But what sayest Thou?"

A long stillness followed, so lengthy the accused woman risked a quick glance at the teacher someone in the crowd had addressed as Jesus. He looked kinder than those who had taken her, but it would avail nothing. A law was a law, not to be broken. She thought bitterly of the man with whom she had been found. Why was he not here, as well? Had those who took her conveniently allowed him to escape?

The silence continued, then a slight rustling sound came from Jesus' robe as He stooped down and with His finger wrote on the ground as though He heard them not.

The prisoner wondered, but the scribes and Pharisees continued railing against her, demanding that Jesus answer.

He stood and said to them, "He that is without sin among you, let him first cast a stone at her." He stooped down again and wrote upon the ground.

The woman's mouth fell open. Little as she knew about Jewish law, she realized Jesus had challenged those who brought her to be judged with the sharpest challenge imaginable. Not that it would benefit her. Some of these self-righteous men considered themselves so holy they wouldn't recognize sin in their hearts if it stung like the desert scorpions.

She tensed, waiting for the first missile to tear into her flesh. Someone coughed. Feet shuffled. She felt movement and raised her head. Jesus still stooped down, busy with writing, but one by one, the scribes and Pharisees stole away.

At last, Jesus arose and faced her. "Woman, where are those thine accusers? Hath no man condemned thee?"

Trembling, unable to believe she alone remained before

Jesus, she stammered, "No man, Lord."

He looked straight into her eyes. She felt He knew everything about her, more than anyone on earth could know. He spoke. "Neither do I condemn thee. Go and sin no more."

When Jesus had gone, she stood alone in the place where her huddled, broken body would have lain if not for Him, still dazed from the strange encounter with even stranger results. Instead of a death sentence, Jesus had given pardon and an admonition: Go and sin no more.

What lay ahead? New life, surely. For once she looked into Jesus' face and beheld His majesty, the past meant nothing; the future, everything.

John 8

blind from birth

Each time her son went forth to beg, his mother's heart ached. Was it not enough that God had cursed him with blindness from birth? Why must he also be forced to beg? She sighed. There was no other choice. She and her husband between them could not earn enough to provide even the rudest shelter, the coarsest food without the pittance the son brought in.

"Better to die and be out of this miserable life," she muttered.

Strange tales came to their household of a teacher said to heal. Neighbors told stories passed on from those who claimed to have stood by and seen Jesus of Nazareth touch the infirm and make them whole. Something stirred within the blind man's mother. She hastily pressed it down. Even Jehovah did not heal those blind from birth. Yet her gnarled hands stilled at her work, and she caught herself dreaming. Suppose. . .

"Nay," she chastised herself. "Such a thing cannot be, although

I am desperate enough to try anything. Perhaps I should seek out this teacher and see for myself if He does the miracles they say."

One day she went to the place where her son sat begging. A little crowd had gathered in front of the spot her son occupied. The mother heard someone ask, "Master, who did sin, this man or his parents, that he was born blind?"

Anguish went through the listening mother. Had she not asked herself the same question as many times as there were stars in the sky? She numbly waited for the answer that would confirm and condemn her.

A rich voice replied, one filled with compassion and authority. "Neither hath this man sinned, nor his parents. But that the works of God should be made manifest in him. . . ."

The woman elbowed her way through a resentful crowd until she stood near her son. She watched the man whose back was to her stoop, spit on the ground, and make clay of the spittle and dirt. She gasped when he anointed the eyes of her blind son and commanded, "Go, wash in the pool of Siloam."

Paralyzed by shock, the mother saw her son struggle to his feet. She watched him make his way to the pool. He splashed water on his face, removing the last bits of clay clinging to his eyes. The next instant a shriek rose to the heavens. "I see!" He leaped in his gladness. "Praise God, I can see!" He ran toward home on feet made fleet by joy.

When his mother arrived, panting from her exertion, her son stood in a circle of neighbors babbling questions, wondering if this were really he who had been blind. The seeing man told what had happened, yet some could not believe this, their neighbor, had received sight. "Where is the One who healed you?" they asked, but the son knew not.

"My son!" His sobbing mother clasped him in her arms, feeling her bitterness vanish when their tears mingled. It gave her strength to face the Pharisees when they came claiming Jesus was a sinner and not of God. Had He not healed on the Sabbath? They did not believe the man had ever been blind. "Is this your son, who ye say was blind? How then doth he now see?"

The glad mother and father stood their ground, although trembling with fear. These religious leaders had agreed that anyone who confessed Jesus was Christ should be put out of the synagogue. They told the questioners their son had indeed been born blind. They could not explain why he now saw. "He is of age; ask him. He shall speak for himself," they told the Pharisees.

Their son reminded them God did not hear sinners; if Jesus were not of God, He could do nothing. The Pharisees cast him out, still mumbling against Jesus, but the little family rejoiced at the restoring of their son.

Jesus later came to the man he had healed. The son believed and worshiped Him. Did the desperate mother and her husband also accept Him as the Son of God? Perhaps, for Jesus healed far more than their son as He passed by.

John 9

stephen, Christian martyr

He had a face like an angel as the false case was brought against him. Stephen, chosen to serve the church in Jerusalem, was charged with preaching against the law of Moses and against God. In reality, Stephen possessed special God-given powers to perform miracles and to speak with wisdom in the name of Christ. He was such an effective speaker that his critics were unable to argue with him. So they plotted lies against him and brought him before the high priest.

When he was asked to defend himself, Stephen spoke eloquently of how God had guided their ancestors. He reminded his listeners how the people of old had revolted against their leader Moses and had angered the Lord by worshiping an idol. He concluded by boldly charging his accusers with breaking Moses' law themselves—and with murdering the Lamb of God, Jesus Christ.

This infuriated them. They became so angry they ground their teeth and covered their ears so they could no longer hear Stephen. A maddened, unreasonable mob finally rushed and seized Stephen.

The brave disciple seemed oblivious to the uproar around him. He lifted his eyes and gazed on a most beautiful vision: the Son of Man, Jesus Christ, standing at the right side of God.

Stephen described what he saw to his tormentors, but it only angered them further. They hustled him outside the city and began throwing rocks at him. Under the deadly barrage, Stephen asked God to receive his spirit. As he fell to his knees, he cried out—as his Savior on the cross had cried out not long before—"Lord, do not count this sin against them." Then he died.

Thus Stephen became the first martyr for Christ. Among the throng of killers was a young man named Saul, who became the most dreaded persecutor of the early church—until his own encounter with the Lord changed him into a steadfast, unflinching Christian martyr like his forerunner, Stephen.

Acts 6:5–8:2

paul, missionary to the roman empire

When Stephen, the first Christian martyr, was stoned to death in Jerusalem, a young man named Saul kept the coats of the men who attacked him. Saul then joined the general effort to eradicate Christ's disciples and became one of the leading persecutors of the early church. He went from house to house, arrested the believers, and threw them in jail.

The Jewish leaders sent Saul to Damascus to arrest Christ's followers there. But on the way, Saul met Jesus. This would have enormous impact on the spread of Christianity.

On the road to Damascus, the Lord appeared to Saul and his companions as a blinding light. "Why are you persecuting Me?" a voice demanded.

"Who are You?" Saul asked.

"It is I, Jesus, the One you are persecuting."

Blinded and trembling, Saul asked, "What do You want me to do?"

Jesus told him to go into Damascus and wait for instructions there.

Meanwhile, the Lord told a believer in Damascus named Ananias to find Saul. Ananias was hesitant because he'd heard of Saul's merciless persecution of the Christians. But he did as God told him.

When Ananias touched Saul, scales fell from the tormentor's eyes so he could see again. Right away Saul was baptized and filled with the Holy Spirit, joined the believers in Damascus, and began preaching with power that astonished the hearers. They knew he'd come to Damascus as an enemy of Christ, not a believer. Not only so, but the Jewish leaders there conspired to kill him. But his Christian friends smuggled him out of the city hidden in a large basket.

Saul returned to Jerusalem. At first, he was rejected by the Christians because of his reputation. They doubted that their former persecutor had sincerely believed in Christ. But through the mediation of a church leader named Barnabas, Saul was accepted and began to help build up the young church. Again the Jewish leaders tried to kill him, and again his new Christian comrades whisked him away to safety.

Saul became a missionary and soon after became known as Paul. He and his companions traveled through the Roman Empire preaching the gospel, encouraging new believers, and teaching the young churches how to worship and conduct their lives as believers. Paul and his companions were the objects of harassment and imprisonment and ultimately were executed for their beliefs. This was a complete role reversal for the one-time persecutor named Saul.

In his journeys through the eastern Mediterranean, Paul lived in constant danger from the Lord's foes and from the uncertainties of travel. Not only was he shipwrecked, but he was jailed and often beaten.

Even in captivity Paul was a powerful witness for Christ. Once Paul and his companion Silas were imprisoned in Philippi because they freed a slave girl from an evil spirit of fortune-telling. Her owners were furious with Paul and Silas because the owners had been using her fortune-telling as a means of making money. They convinced the court to imprison Paul.

Stripped and severely beaten, Paul and Silas were chained deep inside the prison. There, in the middle of the night, the apostles prayed and sang hymns to the other prisoners! Next, God sent an earthquake that shook the prison so violently that the heavy doors fell open and the chains were loosened from the inmates. When the jailer ran to investigate, he thought the prisoners had escaped. The Romans would kill him for this! He was about to commit suicide when Paul stopped him. "Don't worry," Paul told him. "We are all here." The jailer and his entire household believed in Jesus as a result of this event.

Paul was finally sent to Rome for a trial before Caesar Nero. While awaiting trial, Paul continued to preach the gospel for two years while living in a rented house. Scripture does not record his end, but it's assumed that Paul was beheaded in Rome before Nero fell from power in AD 68.

Acts 7:57–28:30; The Letters of Paul

rhoda, excited servant girl

Rhoda, who served in the house of Mary the mother of John Mark, made herself small in the corner and listened to the prayers of those around her.

"We beseech Thee on behalf of our brother Peter," one prayed. "Has not Herod, the king, already killed James, the brother of John? Father, Thou knowest how it pleased those Jews who believe not in Jesus, so much that Herod further took Peter. Even now our beloved brother lies in prison, guarded by many soldiers. Deliver him, O God, that he may bring us Thy word again."

Rhoda fought back tears. She loved the big, rough man Christ had called from his fishing nets to be a fisher of men. When he laughed, her own lips curved upwards. Most of all, she loved hearing Peter's stories about Jesus.

If only she, too, could have walked with the Master! Rhoda found it hard to stay with her duties when Peter came. She longed to sit at his feet every waking hour. Each retold tale of the Christ made the young maiden's heart beat faster.

She silently prayed for Peter. She knew although it was simple and short, the petition would mingle with the prayers of the others in a mighty plea to God.

Ears made keen by service detected a knocking at the gate. Rhoda's heart gave a sickening lurch. Since Herod stretched forth his hands to vex certain members of the church, believers lived with fear. They refused to give up their beliefs and prayers but knew they, like so many others, might be seized.

On slow feet, the damsel went to the gate. "It is Peter," a voice said.

Relief and joy filled her. So glad was she, Rhoda failed to open the gate but ran back inside. "Peter even now stands before the gate," she cried.

Disbelief filled their faces. "Thou art mad," they told her.

"Nay," Rhoda insisted again and again. "I did not mistake his voice."

Those in the house looked at one another. "It is his angel."

The knocking increased. At last they opened the door. They gaped in astonishment. Peter stood outside, face creased by a broad smile. He beckoned with his hand for them to hold their peace, then stepped inside.

"I have much to tell you," he said in the mighty voice that once bellowed orders to his fishing comrades during wild storms. "This same night I lay sleeping between two soldiers, bound with two chains. The keepers before the door kept the prison." Excitement and triumph shone in his eyes.

"I awakened when a light shined in the prison; I thought it a vision. A man stood before me. He smote me on the side and raised me up, saying, 'Arise up quickly.' My chains clanked; I felt their weight lift when they fell from me.

"The man told me to gird myself and bind on my sandals. He ordered me to cast my garment about me and follow him. I obeyed. When we were safely past the first and the second ward, we came unto the iron gate that leadeth into the city. I marveled, for it opened to us of its own accord. We went out and passed on through one street. My companion departed." He hesitated.

Rhoda felt her body tremble. She had seen Peter in many dispositions, but never had his countenance shone brighter. She clasped her hands and waited.

Peter's voice dropped to a whisper. A look of awe came to his face. "I came to myself and realized where I was. I cried, 'Now I know of a surety that the Lord hath sent His angel and hath delivered me out of the hand of Herod and from all the expectation of the people of the Jews.' I came to this house." His eyes twinkled with merriment. "My young sister grew so excited, she left me standing outside the gate."

"In spite of our constant prayers, we did not believe it could really be you," one of the eldest brokenly confessed. "God forgive us! Only this maiden, scarcely past childhood, recognized the truth."

Peter smiled, and Rhoda's heart burned within her. She would never forget this night, not even if she lived beyond the allotted seventy or eighty years* and became an aged, wrinkled crone.

*Psalm 90:10

Acts 12

Lydia of the city of Thyatira was known for her successful selling in the marketplace. Word of her dealings in purple cloth brought to her those from many walks of life. She furnished the finest fabrics to some of the most well-known households in the city, royalty included.

Besides having the high degree of business knowledge needed to compete with other sellers of purple, Lydia possessed an even greater and more precious attribute: She worshiped God.

One Sabbath, she discovered that a much-discussed preacher named Paul intended to pray and speak to the women of the city by a riverside. "I will see for myself what manner of man Paul—once known as Saul, who sought out and persecuted Christians—really is," she told herself.

Seated among the others who flocked to hear, she felt her heart being opened to Paul's message. It burned within her, and when Paul asked for those who believed to come and be baptized, not only she but her entire household came and entered the waters of the river.

Afterward, she besought Paul, saying, "If you have judged me to be faithful to the Lord, come into my house and abide there."

Paul reports, "She constrained us," meaning him and Timothy.

Imagine Lydia's great joy at having them in her home. What stories she and the faithful members of her household must have heard from the determined Paul, who now brought people to Christ even more fervently than he once persecuted them unto death! How many miracles took place within the home she gladly opened to the servant of the Lord? There is no record, but surely the good woman received great blessings in return for her faith and kindness.

Acts 16

Timothy was Paul's trusted associate—a remarkable status for a young man. He was among the first Christian missionaries and was in charge of the church in Ephesus on the coast of Asia Minor. Ephesus had been the scene of a major riot when Timothy visited the city with Paul. Like many other leaders of the early church, Timothy endured persecution and imprisonment.

Paul's first letter to Timothy gave advice and instructions on how to lead a church. Paul warned against unsound teachers, discussed the purpose of worship and the necessary qualities of church elders and deacons, admonished Timothy to use his God-given talents, and advised him how to deal with specific problems and circumstances he would face as a church leader. "Don't be self-conscious about your youthfulness," Paul told Timothy. "Just concentrate on setting a good example by what you say, how you live, your love for people, and your faith in God."

Timothy's second letter from Paul was brief and climaxed with Paul's premonition of his martyrdom. "I have fought the good fight," Paul wrote. "I have finished the race. I have kept the faith."

Paul was in Rome awaiting his trial before Nero when he wrote the letters to Timothy. He implored Timothy and the apostle Mark to join him in Rome. And so perhaps Timothy was present at the martyrdom of the apostle Paul, his father in the faith.

Acts 16:1; 17:14–15; 18:5; Philippians 1:1; 2:19; Colossians 1:1; 1 Timothy; 2 Timothy; Hebrews 13:23

ABOUT THE AUTHORS

colleen l. reece

was born and raised in a small, western Washington logging town. She has written 140 books and was twice voted Heartsong Presents Favorite Author of the Year.

julie reece-demarco

is a multi-published, award-winning author and a practicing attorney and legal educator in Washington State. She has authored many beloved titles.

daniel elton harmon

has written more than fifty books and edits a magazine and newsletter. He lives in Spartanburg, South Carolina. (www.danieleltonharmon.com)

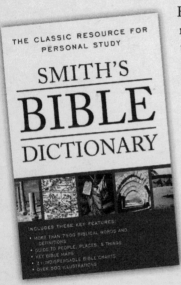